GROW
THE
GOOD
LIFE

GROW
THE
GOOD
LIFE

Why a Vegetable Garden
Will Make You Happy,
Healthy, Wealthy, and Wise

MICHELE OWENS

RODALE

Rodale books may be purchased for business or promotional use or for special sales. For information, please write to:
Special Markets Department, Rodale Inc., 733 Third Avenue, New York, NY 10017

Printed in the United States of America
Rodale Inc. makes every effort to use acid-free ∞, recycled paper ♲.

Book design by Christopher Rhoads

Library of Congress Cataloging-in-Publication Data

Owens, Michele.
Grow the good life : why a vegetable garden will make you happy, healthy, wealthy, and wise / Michele Owens.
    p.   cm.
Includes bibliographical references and index.
ISBN 978–1–60529–589–3   hardcover
1. Vegetable gardening. 2. Backyard gardens. I. Title.
SB321.O94 2010
635—dc22   2010030484

Distributed to the trade by Macmillan
2   4   6   8   10   9   7   5   3   1   hardcover

LIVE YOUR WHOLE LIFE™

We inspire and enable people to improve their lives and the world around them.

For Milo, Georgia, and Grace

CONTENTS

What I've Hauled Out of the Garden

I wrote this book to help people see how easy and how rewarding it is to grow beautiful food. Those ideas seem obvious to me, now that I've spent the last 18 years considering my vegetable garden one of the great joys of my life. However, they are clearly not obvious to many of my neighbors, who look at me with some degree of puzzlement whenever they see me out with my shovel.

America in the early 21st century is definitely *not* a gardening culture, but it may well be on its way to becoming one, and I'd like to give that transformation a definite shove. I hate to think of anybody deprived of such a source of pleasure as a vegetable garden just because he or she doesn't know where to begin.

Let me tell you how I got started. I certainly belonged to the ranks of the super-ignorant when I made my first garden, but it was not a gradual process of enlightenment that turned me into a backyard farmer. It was one single moment of towering pique, at 3:00 p.m. on a miserably cold January afternoon in 1993.

Yes, the ground was frozen, and yes, it would be another 3 months at least before anyone could push the first peas into the earth, but no matter: I was transformed in the dead of winter at the

Grand Union supermarket in the rural village of Cambridge, New York. My husband and I had people coming over for dinner that night, and I was horrified to discover the limits of the produce department in January. My choices were wilted cabbage, rubbery carrots, soft potatoes, or hari-kari.

I was doubly horrified because I'd recently dragged my husband out of New York City, which he loved, and talked him into buying an old house upstate because I needed something I couldn't put my finger on that I couldn't find in New York: light, air, soil, something. We were in our early thirties and married only a few years. Jeff was miserable in the country, so I was miserable.

My beloved husband's grim mood was not all that was getting me down, either. It had taken me a long time to find a job in the uncongenial labor market of Albany, New York, and the one I'd found was with such uniquely seamy people—they'd soon be investigated for running a pyramid scheme—that I shuddered every time I entered their office building. The heating bills for the decrepit 200-year-old house we'd bought because it was cheap and beautiful and had a center hall big enough to drive a truck through were arriving like body blows. The thermometer seemed to be reaching below minus 30 every night, such extreme cold that your nose hairs would freeze instantly the moment you stepped outside.

And the discovery that our sufferings were going to include no food worth eating—well, *that* was just too much for me. A nice dinner at the end of the day is to me what I imagine church on Sunday is to the faithful: the minimum requirement to keep my spirits from dragging entirely on the ground.

"This will not stand," I vowed there in the produce aisle of the

Grand Union, a newly minted revolutionary with a bunch of limp carrots in her fist.

That spring, I made my first garden. I was so stupid about the task at hand that my husband actually had to show me how to use a shovel. Still, I was in such a rage to lay in some decent ingredients for a change that I managed to rip 60 square feet out of the lawn with a pick, an unbelievably arduous job.

I didn't plant much—only the holy triumvirate of basil, tomatoes, and arugula. But they grew and were gorgeous and delicious and gave me beautiful salads and pesto for months. My ambitions were stoked. The next spring, we hired a guy with a tractor to dig a much bigger garden. My husband, a little more used by then to his country exile, bought me a very romantic birthday present—a truckload of mushroom compost—and I was off and running, a full-fledged backyard farmer who rarely ate any vegetable she wouldn't try to grow.

The Grand Union supermarket chain, on the other hand, which condescended so unforgivably to its rural customers, soon entered bankruptcy and then disappeared as a freestanding company. I like to think I had a hand in that.

I started gardening because I wanted better-tasting food, and I certainly took that out of my garden, in floods. What I didn't expect were the many other things I've taken out of my garden besides beautiful meals. I discovered that I loved the exercise of digging and that it made a nagging pain in my shoulder disappear. I loved the way the garden looked. I loved the way it smelled. I got intense pleasure from the creatures who shared my garden—toads, birds, and spectacular yellow and black garden spiders that would set up shop among my greens. I liked the way the seasons followed each other in the garden, each with its own purpose. I liked managing early crops and late crops, with one replacing another like a symphony. After eating my beautiful food, I liked turning the stuff other people threw away—apple cores, carrot ends, potato peelings—into compost that would yield beautiful food again. My garden gave me a profound sense of connection to the whole cycle of life. In the garden, I always felt happy.

The other thing I didn't know when I began was how seamlessly my garden would fit into the normal insanity of modern life. From the time I made my first garden, I not only worked like mad at various jobs, I had three babies, sold my house and bought two others, acquired various cats, dogs, hens, and goldfish—and yet became so slick and efficient as a backyard farmer that every year I produced more food in less time.

In fact, I've taken so much out of my vegetable garden over the years for such limited effort on my part that I've long considered non-gardeners faintly crazy. Now, however, we are arriving as a nation at a political, economic, epidemiological, and environmental moment when it clearly *is* crazy not to grow a little food.

As I write this, we are struggling to emerge from the worst economic downturn since the Great Depression. Millions of jobs have been lost; the values of homes and retirement accounts have plummeted. And food prices, which soared with the oil price spike in 2008, remain high—while a package of vegetable seeds is still one of the world's great bargains.

Of course, money is not the only reason why it makes infinite sense at this particular moment for more of us to become gardeners.

Our current food system represents a fifth of America's fossil fuel consumption, an enormous contributor to the environmental and political anguish associated with this country's carbon habit. Industrial farming's overreliance on artificial fertilizer made from natural gas not only gives every radish a watermelon-sized carbon footprint, but the excess nitrogen from this fertilizer also contributes to greenhouse gas emissions and flows into rivers and oceans, where it causes algae to bloom and fish to die. Commercial farming compromises our water supply by sending pesticides and salts into it—and by consuming enormous amounts of water to make large-scale production possible, for example, in an arid place like California's Central Valley. The giant machines used in farming destroy the structure of the soil by compacting it and lead to erosion. To call industrial farming an ecological disaster is understating the case. Meanwhile, the backyard vegetable garden requires not a drop of oil or grain of artificial fertilizer—absolutely nothing whatsoever out of balance with nature.

It's also increasingly clear that industrial food is making Americans sick and fat. More than a third of adult Americans are now obese, as are 17 percent of children. An appalling 7.8 percent of our population has full-blown diabetes. Leisure hours spent lifting a remote rather than a shovel are not helping matters, either. Even if we didn't produce a lick of food as a result of our labors, we'd all still be better off spending more time working the yard.

In the last few years, we have had an energy crisis, a climate crisis, an obesity crisis, and a financial crisis converging here at home—and cruel food shortages in the developing world caused by increasing pressure on agricultural lands around the globe.

Meanwhile, in this land-rich suburban nation, most of us produce nothing in the backyard but lawn clippings. I'm sorry, that's not just unimaginative of us; it's borderline self-destructive.

The good news here is that growing a little food in the backyard is nothing like taking a vitamin pill, or giving up pasta or beef, or bundling up newspapers for recycling, or replacing incandescent bulbs with ugly compact fluorescents, or forgoing airplane trips, or spending hours on a treadmill, or any other form of virtue as currently defined. It won't shrink your horizons and turn you into somebody duty-driven and humorless, which is, after all, one of the most uncongenial of personality types.

Instead, gardening will expand your horizons in ways that are hard to imagine until you are out in the fresh air and sunshine digging away.

With this book, I hope to spur you to get out and experience that fresh air and sunshine yourself. I won't give you rules for making a garden—I wouldn't presume to dictate something so personal—but I will suggest ways to think about garden-making. Most of all, I will try to describe the many rewards of growing dinner in the backyard, though I know I am condemned only to scratch the surface here.

ONE

Why *Don't* Americans Garden?

On March 20, 2009, the First Lady of the United States did something unprecedented in post–World War II America. She picked up a spade and broke ground for a vegetable garden at the White House. Clearly, this was more of a cultural statement than a physical challenge she'd be taking on personally. Mrs. Obama's attire for the groundbreaking—what appeared to be a dry-clean-only wool sweater and wool pants tucked into fashiony motorcycle boots—was so inappropriate for shovel-work, it made gardeners everywhere smile. But as a statement, that White House garden is just superb. Somebody has to say it: Growing vegetables is a perfectly sensible part of running a household, even a household as elegant as the Obamas'. This is something that clearly has not occurred to most of our countrymen.

In fact, I almost never go for a walk or for a drive without being struck by how many big, sunny yards I see and how very few vegetables I see in them. This is true in rural Washington County, New York, where I lived for a dozen years and where I now have a small weekend house and a big vegetable garden. It's certainly true in the small, lively city of Saratoga Springs, New York, where I lead my weekday existence.

And it's trebly true in suburban Bergen County in the Garden State of New Jersey, where I grew up. Drive down Franklin Turnpike from Ramsey to Allendale on a sunny day in early May, and you will be assaulted by an insane exuberance of lilacs, ornamental cherries, magnolias, and crabapples in bloom—not to mention the cheerfully clashing colors of their flowers. The suburban yards there are lush; the bushes, trees, and grass all green and healthy; the soil clearly excellent; yet in many years of visiting my family, I have stumbled across only two vegetable gardens.

The first was a small one next to an unkempt old house that suggested both an elderly occupant and economic necessity; the second, also small, is maintained by my sister-in-law Na, who is Thai and a professional cook. Unlike her fellow suburbanites, Na comes from a gardening culture, knows it's no big deal to stick a few of her kids' favorite vegetables into the ground, and knows they taste better than what you can buy even in the fanciest supermarket. For years, she worked for organic grocer Whole Foods, but preferred her own vegetables even to what she could buy at a discount there.

Strangely enough, if you want to see vegetable gardens, you might do better in a big city like Detroit or Washington or Boston, where there are real grow-your-own-food movements in neighborhoods largely ignored by supermarket chains and activists who use community gardens to erase urban blight, as well as lots of hip young people who understand the glamour of working the soil.

The United States Department of Agriculture confirms how little backyard farming really occurs in America. It has records dating back to 1869 that consider the dollar value of homegrown food compared to total expenditures on food eaten at home. The last time the nation shopped the backyard for 20 percent of its food by dollar value was 1943. The basic pattern since has been steady decline, and today, we grow just a little more than 1 percent of the food we eat at home. Of course, 1 percent may be on its way to 2 percent, since seed companies have reported dramatically rising sales in recent years. But this is not yet enough of a revolution to satisfy me.

More about that later. First I want to address the *why not* question. Why did the backyard garden, once an important part of most households, nearly disappear by the early years of the 21st century?

Ask any non-gardener, and he or she will tell you it's because growing food is too hard—sweaty and time-consuming and tricky—the kind of thing nobody in his or her right mind would do once the supermarket was invented.

Actually, it's arguably just as sweaty, time-consuming, and tricky to navigate crowded roads in a car in order to arrive at some cavernous supermarket and push a cart around its miles of aisles a few times a week. And the supermarket is certainly a less pleasant experience.

I'd argue that the main reason we don't grow food is because our parents and grandparents didn't.

Sure, they patriotically tended their Victory Gardens during World War II, easing pressure on the food supply and allowing the government to feed the troops more cheaply. The USDA estimates that in 1943, 20 million Victory Gardens produced 40 percent of the country's fresh vegetables. My father, who grew up in the most urban way possible in Astoria, Queens—playing stickball in the streets and dragging a mattress out onto a fire escape on sweltering summer nights—vividly remembers working the Victory Garden at the Catholic school he attended as a class assignment.

But when the war was over, the culture actively turned against such humble labors. For people who grew up amidst the privations of the Great Depression, followed by the privations or outright horrors of war, *nothing* was more seductive than the idea of leaving the old ways behind.

My mother is a prime example. She grew up in Germany on a particularly charmless small farm in a particularly charmless small house—dark, low-ceilinged, and since the stalls are attached to the house, full of nasty flies and a powerful smell of manure. She also grew up at a moment when living on a farm did not mean you wouldn't nearly starve to death, since most of the food her parents produced was earmarked for Hitler's soldiers. My mother still shudders at the memory of nothing to eat but lard on stale bread and the atmosphere of terror as bombers whined overhead and the Gestapo staged unannounced inspections that threatened to have her father dragged away. It was not comparable in misery to what Jewish children were suffering at the same moment, but it was not blithe either.

The war ended when she was 12, and when she got the chance to go away to the city to school the next year, she took off like a rocket and never looked back. In her twenties, she came to New York City, and in her early thirties, moved to New Jersey, where she settled in suburban splendor, with a gold velvet couch, creamy wool wall-to-wall carpeting, and a leather-seated luxury car to convey her from place to place.

Though our first suburban house had a yard of almost 2 acres, including a sunny, flat spot perfect for a vegetable garden, my mother did not garden. I remember her going once, and just once, to pick up a bushel basket of manure at the last surviving dairy farm in our suburbanizing town because she wanted to grow some rhubarb. Though rhubarb is one of the most indestructible of edible plants, it barely lasted a year before she mowed it over. The manure may have finished the endeavor off. I think my mother's whole adult life has been about putting the greatest possible distance between herself and a shovelful of manure.

Even those people who spent World War II on the comparatively comfortable American home front were ready to begin anew when the war ended. They'd endured the Great Depression, when the country's poorest could be seen eating out of garbage cans. They'd had to adjust to life without their young men, who went off to war by the millions. After May of 1942, they'd had to adapt to food rationing, too, so the government had what it needed to supply its soldiers and sailors.

Of course, as Harvey Levenstein points out in his book *Paradox of Plenty: A Social History of Eating in Modern America*, rationing hardly represented deprivation: Americans were asked to survive on about 2½ pounds of meat per person per week, while the British got just a pound and the Russians almost no meat at all. And of course, thanks to the Victory Gardens, there was a bounty of fresh vegetables. My father tells me that his urban working-class family never lacked for anything during the war. If they didn't have a ration coupon for some food, it could easily be bought on the black market.

Nonetheless, since rationing inspired a black market, protests, hoarding, and conspiracy theories, it's clear that Americans at least *felt* deprived.

The deprivations of the war also included a severe housing shortage. Beginning in the early '40s—inspired, I am sure, by impending separation and the dangers the men would soon be facing—young couples began reproducing at a startling rate. There had been very little new housing built since the onset of the Great Depression, so by 1947, six million families were shoehorned into the households of relatives and friends, and more were struggling along in temporary housing or places that were absurdly small.

Since the GI Bill guaranteed low-interest loans on new homes, these young families exploded out of the cities into the suburbs by the millions as soon as developers could slap together the Capes and ranches to house them. Many of them now owned their first bit of ground that gave them a chance to grow their own food. Only they didn't.

The developers of the new suburban communities that sprang up to house these postwar families encouraged passivity towards the landscape in their customers. They installed not just the houses, streets, trees, and lawns, but the community gathering spaces as well, such as shops, playgrounds, parks, even churches. They also put in place the rules to enforce uniformity in this landscape, with the Levitts of Levittown fame micromanaging the landscape down to the point of prohibiting clotheslines and mowing any unmowed lawns long after the houses were sold—and sending their more slovenly homeowners the bill.

Though the homeowner's guide for the Pennsylvania Levittown

includes pages and pages of micro-instructions for lawn and shrub care, vegetable gardens are never once mentioned. "Mow your lawn and remove weeds at least once a week between April 15th and November 15th," the guide demands. "Nothing makes a lawn—and a neighborhood—and a community—look shabbier than uncut grass and unsightly weeds."

The truth is that all this aesthetic consistency and shabbiness-prevention suited young American families just fine. They were not interested in scrabbling for a living with chickens in the backyard. The country had been scrabbling for two decades, and they were heartily sick of it. They wanted to move from air-conditioned cars to air-conditioned houses as clean as spaceships—to lead lives that were pristine and factory-made. Since World War II, America has defined progress as *any* development that holds the natural world at a genteel remove.

Since there was considerable money to be made off of people determined to have done for them things they once would have done for themselves—including producing much of their own food—new businesses instantly sprang up to serve them. The self-service supermarket, which had been invented decades earlier, only really took off after the war. And what really characterized these supermarkets was the startling array of packaged "convenience foods" they were now selling, now that home refrigerators began to include a freezer compartment and a new car-based suburban life encouraged less frequent shopping and more reliance on the already preserved and prepared.

Of course, "convenience" was not a postwar invention. In the final volume of his brilliant intellectual history of America, *The*

Americans: The Democratic Experience, Daniel J. Boorstin notes how many means of transporting and preserving food were invented or perfected here in America. By the mid-19th century, the railroads were being used to bring out-of-season produce to New York City. By 1858, Gail Borden had perfected the canning of condensed milk, inspired by pity for the Donner party, pioneers who were forced to eat their dead companions while snowed in for a winter in the Sierra Nevada. By 1881, Gustavus Franklin Swift's advances in refrigerated railroad cars allowed the shipment of dressed beef from Chicago to the Eastern cities even in the summer. And by the 1920s, Clarence Birdseye was working on a quick-freezing method for superior frozen food.

Boorstin characterizes this inventiveness in food preservation as one example of the relentless force of American democracy: "The flavor of life had once come from . . . the special taste and color of each season's diet. The American democracy of times and places meant making one place and one thing more like another by bringing them under the control of man."

It's the nature of our economy. Here in America, name any luxury—including the incomparable luxury of a fragrant strawberry in season—and some clever entrepreneur will eventually find a way to bring it to everybody at any moment.

Never mind that the strawberry may well have given up that fragrance in the process of being packaged, transported, and sold. Never mind that many convenience foods tasted horrible, so lifeless and colorless that by 1958, an arsenal of 704 chemicals was used to manipulate foods that had already been manipulated into pablum. But taste was never the point of convenience foods—clearly not.

It's questionable even whether time saved was the point: Is jarred mayonnaise really faster than the vastly tastier stuff that can be made in a blender in 30 seconds? Is a pancake mix really faster than throwing flour, eggs, milk, oil, and baking powder together in a bowl? Economist Valerie Ramey of the University of California at San Diego has found that per capita, the time adults spent on housework in the United States hardly altered at all during the 20th century, despite the explosion in labor-saving electric appliances and prepared foods. The time that before the war might have been spent gardening and cooking fresh foods, after the war was devoted to less life-affirming and creative pursuits like hauling one's car and one's tired ass to the market.

And certainly, money saved was not an argument for convenience foods over homecooked and homegrown. In *Paradox of Plenty,* Levenstein points out that by the 1930s, even in rural areas, processed factory foods were considered more desirable than local foods: " . . . Even those who could little afford them sacrificed to purchase them. Poor Appalachian farmers shunned tasty country hams in favor of water-logged canned ones; they sold homegrown vegetables to buy the brand-name canned variety."

Convenience foods stole a lot of flavor out of a lot of lives, not to mention the joyful experience of garden-making. But they did clearly offer something meaningful in return, or no one would have bought them: They made one part of the modern world. And that was why even the poorest farmers wanted to eat them. In a country made up of all kinds of outliers, from new immigrants to lonely farmers in lonely hollows, adopting national brands was a way of belonging.

Of course, my mother was one of those eccentric immigrants. But to her infinite credit, she was too stubborn to be wooed by the call of the advertiser. In fact, she thought that the way Americans ate was *insane*. She shopped farm stands and bakeries; she bought eggs from the ancient deaf lady down the street who lived without electricity or running water; and she refused to allow me and my brothers to grow up on the prepared foods that built my friends' strong bodies 12 ways. In my childhood home, there was no Wonder Bread, no Ragú spaghetti sauce, and no Twinkies. There was only crusty bakery rye, homemade spaghetti sauce with meatballs full of garlic and fresh herbs, and pound cakes made from scratch. So she made me eccentric, too, and I was both bitter about that as a child and also slightly aglow from the quality of the food I ate.

Even though the Greatest Generation and Silent Generation were followed by more environmentally clued-in generations with more mature notions of progress—and a greater appreciation for interesting food—there has never been a widespread revival of the kitchen garden. While the Arab oil embargo and rising food prices did inspire a back-to-the-garden movement in the mid-1970s, that movement was barely a blip on the USDA "Food at Home" chart. And it was certainly not a robust enough revolution to make a dent in the suburb I grew up in. I was a bored middle schooler wandering a lot of backyards at that stage, so I can assure you that in my town at least, there were no vegetable gardens. Zero.

Why, if growing vegetables is as enjoyable as I claim, did vegetables never return to the backyard stage in a big way?

Simply because there were too few vegetable gardens left to suggest the possibilities to younger people, and too few old sages to teach them how to garden. If ever there were a cultural activity that rewards continuity across the generations, it is gardening. If you have no one to teach you how to cook, for example, trial and error represents nothing more painful than a few terrible meals. In vegetable gardening, if you have to go it alone—and without a writer of the stature of Julia Child to help you—trial and error might cost an entire season's labor and also be very depressing to look at along the way.

The very best advice in gardening comes from old sages, since all gardening, like all politics, is local. While the fundamentals of vegetable growing are simple and universal, the interactions between a particular crop and a particular place and climate are highly variable. So what to plant and when to do it—these are the kinds of things best understood and communicated by thoughtful neighbors.

Today, the few old sages in the field of vegetable gardening—some of whom happen to be young and attractive—are in such demand that they are renting themselves out as gardening coaches. Joshua Wenz, for example, has a Washington, DC–based business called My Organic Garden that builds and maintains backyard vegetable gardens. He finds that his gardens' owners, however, increasingly want coaching from him rather than full-service maintenance. Josh, who grew up in Nebraska, came from a gardening culture: "My dad says that when he was 5 years old, he just went out to the garden where his mother was working and started helping her. It was an unspoken thing. Growing up, I just assumed you had a garden, though I saw it as more of a chore than a source of enjoyment."

Then Josh did some time with the Peace Corps in Bulgaria,

where even in the cities, people grew their own food and relaxed in their gardens. Many of them had small villas in the country, where they eagerly repaired to their vegetable beds and vineyards. Even within the urban centers, there were fruit trees everywhere, and goats in city courtyards. Josh was enchanted and inspired. "I thought, we've got backyards in DC. This is something that can be done here. I put up flyers and tried to figure out a price for helping people over the steep learning curve."

Here is the beauty of the American economy demonstrated once more: Every luxury eventually makes its way out into the wider market, including the luxury of advice from an experienced vegetable gardener.

Now, we arrive at my second explanation for why so few people have grown food crops in the backyard in the last half-century: the horrible way gardening is marketed. If you have to take your information from garden suppliers rather than somebody a generation ahead of you who loves his or her crops, what conclusions can you draw?

If you have to shop the Big Box stores, as I do in Saratoga Springs, given the lack of good independent nurseries near me, you might easily decide that gardening is only for the foolish and the brave. Wander past the rat traps and cockroach killers in Lowe's or Home Depot towards the gardening aisles—these merchants always assume that vermin and gardening are related subjects—and the experience is not unlike that of watching Fox News. You will instantly be riled up into a state of paranoia by people who think that's the best way to keep you interested.

"Defend what's yours: your family, home, and yard." Is this an argument for unauthorized wiretaps or the torture of suspected terrorists or abolishing the estate tax? No, actually, it's the slogan of Ortho, one of the weed-and-pest-control brands owned by ScottsMiracle-Gro. An Ortho sub-brand for another range of products is even blunter: The name of the line is "Total Kill."

In the gardening aisle, the enemy wears many faces. But whatever shape villainy takes—whether that of an ant, a grub, a beetle, a fungus, a deer, or a broad-leafed weed—you can be sure that it will be blown up to a threatening size on the bottle or bag of chemicals being sold for control.

Yes, Lowe's, Home Depot, and Wal-Mart offer a handful of organic products that purport to work in harmony with nature. No, they are not the dominant feature of these gardening centers. Battle is. The colors of the bottles piled to the ceiling and the big paper sacks stacked on the floor like sandbags in trench warfare are aggressively military: dark green, red, gray, yellow. In the backyard garden, apparently, we have to destroy nature in order to save it.

Other pesticide and herbicide companies, preferring a less emotional approach to total control in the garden, take a more pharmaceutical tack. We're not killing stuff, we're curing disease. Spectracide's fungal control product is named "Immunox," in the best bland tradition of pharmaceutical nomenclature. The Bayer Group, whose cross within circle logo will always be associated with the most benign of medicines, aspirin, is also a big player in the pesticide market under the brand Bayer Advanced.

It's not just the branding that's unpleasant in the gardening aisles; it's the subliminal cues, too. There is a gardening store near me, part of a local chain that really should know better, that is impossible to enter without being knocked off your feet by the stench of chemicals. Terrorists make bombs out of chemical fertilizer. You can smell that possibility in this store. Add to the fertilizer a few hundred sacks of grub killer and the regular application of insecticides on the houseplants for sale, and the resulting fragrance is so flinty, astringent, and brimstonelike, it's like visiting a loading dock in hell. Every time I go there to buy twine or a tomato stake, I have to fight the impulse to immediately flee.

Even if you are not the kind of person who instinctively distrusts the products made in insecticide factories, life is enough of a battle in modern America. Who wants to take up a hobby that requires us to gird our loins and become soldiers of the hose and sprayer, or put on rubber gloves and a mask and minister to the inherent sickness of nature? It all just sounds so ulcer-inducing.

What these merchants won't tell you, of course, is that you can happily garden for decades without once employing any of their big guns. Well-managed vegetable gardens are not often besieged by anything that can't be fenced out or picked off. They are *healthy*.

Of course, there are more organic purveyors that cater to more ecologically sensitive gardeners and take a cheerier tone. Yet even these merchants offer so many soil amendments, pest remedies, and specialized tools that trying to keep them straight could make your head spin: tomato fertilizer, pea inoculant, bat guano, milky spore disease, beneficial nematodes, red plastic mulches, row covers, dormant oils. To win the gardener's money, they sell the idea that vegetable gardening demands very precise tools, and therefore precise skills, precise knowledge, and a lot of wearying attention. As a marketing strategy, this is killing the golden goose to get the eggs.

What these merchants won't tell you is how little equipment is really required. Years of vegetable gardening have turned me into a complete minimalist who uses nothing besides shovel, seeds, and mulch. Admittedly, there is very little profit in that message.

Only the very best merchants—and these are few and far between—actually sell *gardening,* which to my mind is all about beautiful seeds, beautiful seedlings, beautiful fruit trees and shrubs, and beautiful structures for plants such as pole beans that need them. Gardening is about sticking stuff in the ground, standing back, and watching it do its beautiful thing, not about fretting about problems that may never arise.

Of course, if you had a yen to make a vegetable garden, and both your neighbors and the merchants failed to help you begin, you could always turn to books. Now we arrive at the third reason our landscape is so innocent of gardens: the incredibly off-putting literature of vegetable growing.

I really feel for the beginner trying to learn gardening from books. But let me say in defense of those many how-to writers of the last half century who have driven so many would-be gardeners into scrapbooking instead, that vegetable gardening is not a natural subject for how-to.

It's a principle-, not a rule-based activity. The principles are so simple—give your crops lots of sun, fertile soil, and sufficient water—that they would hardly fill a page or two, let alone a book. The specific interactions, on the other hand, between a crop, a spot, a climate, and a human personality are so infinitely various that any collection of rules is inevitably contingent and incomplete.

The problem is that many gardening how-to's refuse to admit

the contingency of their own advice. Many of them spend so much time trying to cover every eventuality and anticipating every possible problem that a beginner might reasonably conclude that growing food is nothing *but* a series of problems.

For example, the first piece of advice is usually, "Send your soil off to a lab to be tested," as if the vegetable garden were a delicate chemistry experiment rather than a partnership with nature that's generally proved successful for the last 10,000 years. By all means, test your soil if you suspect lead or industrial waste—but otherwise? I know a lot of serious gardeners and not a *single one* has ever had his or her soil tested.

Authoritative charts are also very popular in vegetable gardening how-to's. Possibly it indicates some deficiency in my intelligence that such charts make my eyes roll back in my head. Possibly it's because I know how irrelevant their information is to a real garden. You might find a chart of the pH preferences of various plants. It might make a beginner reasonably conclude that vegetables are extremely fussy—when most of them will grow in normal garden soil, in a range between slightly acid and slightly alkaline. You might find a similar chart about the water needs of particular vegetables. Again, this is useless information that seems designed only to provoke anxiety in the beginner. No one sets up rain gauges all over the garden and waters each crop by hand in order to hit some theoretical sweet spot. Common sense is sufficient here. Is the soil dry? Water. Have you just had a soaking rain? Don't.

Elaborate charts of planting times are also highly dubious. March in upstate New York and March in Southern California are not the same month. And encyclopedic considerations of pests and diseases belong in encyclopedias in my opinion, not in how-to's, because well-managed gardens are not often sick.

Even if you ignore all this pseudoscientific padding, it's challenging to learn to be a vegetable gardener in one gulp from a book, because finding what really works for you requires a voyage of self-discovery as much as anything. What do you like to do? What are you willing to do? What do you *really* want for dinner?

Yet the how-to's often take a dictatorial tone that is intended to make beginners fall in line. Sometimes the dictator sounds like a cheerleader, but is a dictator nonetheless. Some of them are written by market growers who will inevitably be concerned about very different things than a home gardener, such as large yields, steady production throughout the season, and unblemished produce that will sell. These people are systematizers—it's a job requirement if you are going to make a living feeding hundreds of people a season. So they promote the system that works for them, down to the specific tool for weeding or the pounds of fertilizer per hundred square feet, as the answer to life, the universe, and everything.

Honestly, there are as many routes to happiness in a vegetable garden as there are in life, though it is only the rarest how-to that will admit that. I may find her a little fussy in delineating the requirements of specific crops, but I will always have a soft spot for Barbara Damrosch and her 20-year-old *The Garden Primer* because she is mature enough to consider choices and alternatives, and describes her own practices with a lovely humility of tone. "I am the first to admit," she writes, "that I have my own idiosyncratic approach when it comes to gardening. . . . I read as much as time allows about scientific advances in horticulture, and I'm usually willing to try something new, but most of what I do has come from just plain experience."

Me, too.

It's also clear that no matter how certain a how-to author sounds, his or her advice probably reflects the moment as much as the eternal truths. In the early '90s, when I was a beginning gardener, even in books with an organic bent, there was still a great emphasis on sprays and powders for every problem. Today, the how-to literature seems to be well past that point and able to take a more holistic—and in my opinion, intelligent—view of what constitutes health in a garden.

I also began my gardening career by absorbing a lot of advice about improving the quality of one's soil, which is sound. Most vegetables are annual crops that require rich soil for their explosive growth, and every year, the gardener removes a lot of nutrients from that soil by eating them for dinner. But the advice for improving soil in the early '90s was highly traditional in that it largely focused on messing with it.

An annual tilling, either by hand or with one of those loud and frightening motorized tillers, was advised to make life easier for vegetable roots by pulverizing a path for them. Never mind that the horrors of the Dust Bowl in the 1930s were caused by overtilling, which ruined the structure of fragile prairie soils and allowed the topsoil simply to blow away.

Even better, I learned from books, was double digging. Double digging involves loosening and enriching the soil 2 entire feet deep and moving it in layers. Whether used just to make the garden or—

horrors!—as a regular program, it is ridiculously laborious, the one single piece of advice that has probably driven more would-be backyard farmers screaming out of the garden than any other. Just try digging 400 square feet of ground 2 feet deep in rocky or clay-ridden soil. Before you recommend something like this, in my opinion, you'd better be damned sure that it's necessary.

Yet in terms of actual science, there is no conclusive proof that double digging increases yields. Double digging and other forms of intensive tilling are almost certainly counterproductive because they destroy the structures built up by the life underground that creates healthy soil—the worm tunnels, the root runs, the amazing mycelia or threadlike networks of fungi whose fruits are mushrooms.

Today, you will find books such as Patricia Lanza's *Lasagna Gardening* advocating no tilling at all and instead enriching the soil from the top with layers of organic mulch. Whatever the virtues of this idea in terms of soil science (and there are many), it at least has the virtue of being a garden-making method that might be attempted by someone with a day job.

The truth is that up until now, vegetable gardening gurus have been forced to rely on tradition and their own experience, which may or may not be helpful in your yard, because they have not had the benefit of a tremendous amount of scientific research to help them refine their advice.

Dr. Jeff Gillman, who *is* a scientist, a horticulturalist at the University of Minnesota who has brought a certain delightful scientific skepticism to gardening advice in his books *The Truth about Organic Gardening* and *The Truth about Gardening Remedies*, explains the lack of science in gardening: "Most research at universities is state or federally funded. What the federal government is interested in is feeding the country and the world—not in what's happening in your backyard. So a lot of recommendations were based on research done for big agriculture, not the backyard."

The problem is that industrial agriculture and the backyard garden have entirely different goals. And other scientists use far less temperate language than Dr. Gillman in describing the ways in which universities and government agencies like the United States Department of Agriculture have skewed crop research towards the interests of Big Ag. If you want to make a soil biologist or horticulturalist swear, ask him or her why home food growers haven't gotten better guidance.

"Even many of the varieties we use are based more on industry rather than what will do well in a backyard," Dr. Gillman offers. "Apples, for example, are bred for flavor, storage, and appearance, but for the most part, they haven't been selected for disease resistance." And disease resistance may well be the *most* important quality to a backyard orchardist, who probably has no interest in embarking on an elaborate spraying program.

Dr. Gillman says that the picture is improving with increasing government funding for research into organic agriculture, as the market for organic foods expands and there is increasing interest in sustainable farming that doesn't rely on fossil fuels. "The nice thing is that a lot of organic ideas apply to smaller growers and will be more transferable to gardens."

As a beginning vegetable gardener, I quickly came to the conclusion that many of the practices I saw recommended in books—double digging to make the garden, testing the soil and carefully adding the right amendments, an annual tilling, paying careful attention to the individual requirements of every vegetable and side-dressing particular ones with fertilizer at particular stages of their growth—were so time-consuming, I'd never be able to live up to this ideal.

Despite the fact that I hauled massive amounts of delicious food out of a garden that was utterly beautiful to look at, I spent my first years feeling like a second-rater. If only I had time to side-dress the broccoli, then I'd be a *real* gardener! At some point, I woke up and realized that my garden was fantastically productive. Not one of these recommended practices was in any way necessary, not in my yard.

Ask Josh Wenz, the professional coach, what one idea he feels he needs to convey to beginners, and he offers the classic organic movement advice, "Feed the soil and not the plants." In other words, focus on the context and the details will take care of themselves. Ask another kind of professional, my friend Martha Culliton, a chef, cookbook writer, and true scholar of food, the first piece of advice she'd give on making a kitchen garden, and you'll find an even more relaxed point of view: "Disturb a piece of earth and throw some seeds on it. You'll get food."

It is not hard to garden. That's not to say that you can't spend a lifetime refining your methods and learning the subtleties of particular crops. But it is not hard to begin.

The truth is that Americans don't garden, for the most part, for *cultural* reasons, not for any other kind of reason. In the last few generations, the culture has constantly insinuated that gardening is difficult and inconvenient and wouldn't we rather just get in our cars instead and drive to buy food made in a factory? And en masse, we bought this argument, until growing one's own food seemed entirely irrelevant to a modern life.

Well, it's long past time to seize the idea of convenience *back* from those generations that gave us such meaningless innovations as the electric can-opener and battery-powered knife; back from those people for whom dinner was something made by stirring one convenience food into another; back from those people who knocked down historic urban neighborhoods all over America to build highways that would truck tasteless food to us from across the continent, because it was convenient.

It's time to add some sense of value to our domestic life beyond merely time and labor saved. Here is what's really convenient: ending a workday by wandering out into the yard and seeing what's good for dinner right there, instead of having to get into a car to explore that supremely unpleasant landscape called a supermarket. Here's what's convenient: having ingredients at hand that are so good in themselves, they will more than make up for your limitations as a cook. Here's what's convenient: not worrying about what's been sprayed on your food or what pathogens might be on them. Here's what's really convenient: enjoying that piece of paradise called your yard.

To my mind, it's a shame that so many people should miss out on such a life-affirming, healthy, and pleasurable activity as growing their own dinner, just because it once fell out of fashion.

But fashions change. That's what makes them fashions. And seed companies that range from the mainstream W. Atlee Burpee to the friendly, organic-oriented cooperative Fedco reported dramatically rising sales in recent years. Now we have the White House adding a new luster to the idea of the kitchen garden. We also have a new generation of farmers at the farmers' markets who are young, college educated, hyper-gourmet, and hyperaware of their environmental impact. They have put an attractive face on vegetable growing even for the middle-aged and made it something people want to be near. As architect and urban planner Andrés Duany has declared, "Agriculture is the new golf."

We can hear the cultural wheel turning, squeakily, back to a recognition that backyard farming makes sense, in part because writers like Michael Pollan in the superb *The Omnivore's Dilemma* have dramatized the true weirdness of industrial food production, in part because BP has provoked a new understanding of the environmental costs of fossil fuel use, and in part because you have to be CEO of an oil company to afford to buy nice organic vegetables these days.

In fact, money is a particularly persuasive reason to garden, and that is the subject of my next chapter.

TWO

Money

Better Than Berkshire Hathaway Stock Bought in '65

This is a very interesting moment in the history of American eating.

We've long considered cheap and abundant food a national birthright. After all, this country has a lot of land for farming and much of it is very fertile. We've been food exporters since the 1850s. We were early adopters of industrial methods of farming here in America, too, since manpower was generally scarcer than cropland. And factory farming, with its emphasis on efficiency, efficiency, efficiency, has been very easy on our wallets.

The USDA produces a chart of food expenditures as a share of disposable personal income that shows a steady decline since World War II. While Americans spent almost a quarter of their disposable income on food at the postwar high in 1947, that number has dropped, bit by bit, to less than 10 percent in recent years.

Then came a shock to the system in 2008, when grocery prices soared in tandem with the price of oil. According to the USDA, this was the most substantial increase in grocery prices since 1990. Suddenly, it was no longer unusual to drop items costing $4 or $5 each into the cart at the supermarket. Always more expensive, the superior local and organic alternatives began to seem unaffordable even to the affluent. In late 2008 and 2009, same-store sales fell at natural grocer Whole Foods, and the chain both scaled back its expansion plans and tried to alter its "Whole Paycheck" reputation by emphasizing value.

Even when oil fell from its record high of $147.27 a barrel in July of 2008 to less than $50 a barrel a few months later and the economic downturn became really grim in late 2008, food prices did not instantly fall. Economists call food prices "sticky," which means that once lifted up by rising costs, they tend to stay on the ceiling for a long time before coming down. Today, even after several years of recession, the weekly grocery bill is still likely to be pretty hefty if you have a handful of mouths to feed at home.

Whatever happens to oil and the economy in the short term, there is no reason to expect that the trend towards more expensive food will reverse itself in the long term. It's clear that the global demand for oil is increasing and that the supply is not infinite. And high grocery prices in 2008 were not just due to oil, but also to increasing demand driven by the newly middle class in many emerging economies and the diversion of increasing amounts of cropland to biofuels and animal feed.

The population is rising, crop yields are growing only slowly, and climate change is expected to increase drought in many parts of the world, including food-exporting regions such as southern Europe and western Australia. Marshall Burke, a researcher at the University of California at Berkeley, has developed an economic model that suggests that even a 1°C rise in temperatures could yield a 30 percent rise in grain prices globally by 2030, if the temperature change is abrupt and crops adapt poorly to it.

So what can you do about any of this? Matthew R. Simmons, investment banker to the energy industry, offered *Fortune* magazine one particularly apt piece of advice for navigating an uncertain future: "Grow food in your backyard."

Plant a vegetable garden. It delivers the kind of returns that make hedge fund managers green with envy. Here is just one of many examples from my own garden: A package of organic seeds of my favorite pole bean, 'Blue Coco', sets me back $1.50 every spring. For that sum of money, I can pick a shopping bag full of the most delicious purple string beans every week for at least 8 weeks. At farmers' market prices, each shopping bag holds about $30 worth of beans. So that's $240 worth of produce from a $1.50 investment, a 16,000 percent return over the course of the summer, a Jack and the Beanstalk–scale return where a handful of seeds gives you a ladder to the giant's treasury.

W. Atlee Burpee, America's biggest garden seed company, has certainly scented a marketing opportunity here. In late 2008, it released the results of a 10-year study that showed that a 1-to-25 ratio of costs to benefits in a vegetable garden is a reasonable expectation. According to Burpee, spend $100 on seeds and fertilizer, and you can grow $2,500 worth of herbs and vegetables.

That ratio does not sound outrageous to me. I spend about $200 every year on seed and seedlings, but then, I'm a profligate experimenter who buys five times as many seeds as she needs just to try stuff. I don't buy fertilizer, but I do buy a few hundred dollars' worth of mulch, though in some years, I'll get it from a neighbor for free. In return, I save at least $100 a week on my grocery bill for an 8-month period between May and the end of December. After that, there are still vegetables in the freezer and in the cellar until spring. And if I were more diligent about processing the insane harvest I get in the fall or set up a simple hoop-house—a passive solar greenhouse covered in plastic that would protect the hardiest crops in winter—I could easily carry those savings along throughout the year.

However, money is as funny a question in the garden as it is in every other area of life. One man's extravagance is another man's dire necessity.

The cliché about kitchen gardening is that it's like most hobbies—no matter what the gross value of the end result, the start-up and maintenance costs plus the inexperience of the hobbyist yield little net. William Alexander's 2006 memoir *The $64 Tomato* makes this argument with particular bitterness. Alexander adds up what he spent building his garden and arrives at the eye-popping figure of $16,565, which he amortizes over the handful of Brandywine tomatoes he collects for his efforts at $64 apiece.

Of course, Alexander began this garden in rather lordly fashion by hiring a landscape architect and terracing a slope and installing irrigation in each of 22, count 'em, garden beds. While Alexander never delves deeply into the psychology behind such overkill, he does admit that it is overkill: "People hire landscape architects to design entire landscapes, or patio and pool plantings, or civic gardens. Who hires a professional to figure out where to put the tomatoes? You put down some railroad ties and throw down a few seeds, right? Not us."

That's right. The money you spend making your garden says more about *you* than it does about the nature of vegetable gardening, because it's certainly possible to make a lovely vegetable garden for a few hundred dollars. Michelle Obama recently told a group of schoolkids that the White House garden cost $180 in materials in its first year—and by its first fall had yielded more than 700 pounds of food. You can spend even less if you have a talent for scrounging.

Riet Schumack, for example, who gardens in one of the poorest neighborhoods in America's poorest big city, Detroit, jokes that her vegetable garden is made of "nothing but old debris." Like Alexander, she's gardening on a hillside, only she's terraced it with found materials—stone, brick, old cement blocks. "It's very dramatic," she says in a flat, undramatic Midwestern tone. "I don't want to be prideful, but the whole city talks about my garden. Nobody's seen anything like it." She manages to feed a family of eight out of this garden, by the way, with enough to give away, spending almost nothing on it.

Whenever I protest, however, that writers like Alexander give people the wrong idea about growing food, my husband suggests that I am the *worst* possible argument for the economy of the kitchen garden, given that I now garden at a weekend house, and indeed, *own* the weekend house largely so I can have a big vegetable garden. "Your book should be called *The $200,000 Tomato*," he says when he most wants to annoy me.

Setting aside the cost of that mortgage and the many strange compromises one makes in a long marriage when one side is a frustrated farmer and the other a frustrated Manhattanite, my garden delivers fantastic earnings on minimal operating costs. And clearly, it's possible to make a vegetable garden a net plus in simple economic terms, as there are now suburbanites and urbanites actually supplementing their incomes by farming their yards.

A company called SPIN (that's an acronym for small-plot-intensive) that sells production advice to small market growers estimates that a 2,500-square-foot garden can generate $7,150 worth of food a year. Now that's a serious-sized garden, but even a garden 20 percent of that size will pay for itself fairly quickly, if you can stop yourself from buying 18th-century English statuary to ornament the joint.

So let's talk about planning, making, and maintaining a vegetable garden for the maximum returns of flavor, beauty, and cash equivalents. You will need some capital to begin, and not just money, but also land, labor, and time.

The most essential investment, obviously, is a bit of land. It doesn't have to be big, but it does have to be sunny. Certain leafy crops like lettuces may limp along in semishade—as well as those fruits that grow as understory bushes in nature, such as raspberries and blackberries—but in my experience, even vegetables that don't like heat need a full day of sun.

This is the one requirement in vegetable gardening that cannot be gotten around. If you are really serious about growing food in a shady yard, take down some trees—or move.

Other obstacles are easier to overcome. If the only appropriate spot you've got has poor soil or bad drainage, those can be dealt with by raising or lowering the grade, or employing the gardener's miracle cure: adding lots of organic matter to the soil, such as composted manure, kitchen compost, ground-up leaves, straw, grass clippings, or wood chips. My current garden borders on a bog, which no how-to would ever recommend, yet it is a raging success. I keep adding waves of organic matter to the top of the soil, so the surface of the garden is now rising a bit above-ground level and becoming light and fluffy. I water less there than I would in another garden, too. In a really rainy year, some of my late crop of potatoes might rot in the ground. But in a dry year, I'll take my garden and its happy plants over any high and dry site any day.

Depending on your climate, you may even be able to garden in a spot where you don't have irrigation of any kind. Of course, you really are at the mercy of God if you can't set up a sprinkler, but God is often merciful.

Another limitation on the land front that shouldn't discourage you is not having much of it. The standard advice for beginning gardeners is "go small," and it's not bad advice. An awful lot of food can be grown in a compact, well-managed space, which is why urban farming and community gardening have both exploded in recent years. I once spoke with a woman from Bangladesh who grows not only enough exotic gourds in a 6- by 10-foot plot in the Fenway in Boston to supply her own curries, but enough to broaden her neighbors' culinary horizons as well. My first garden was the same size, and it yielded so much arugula, tomatoes, and basil that my husband and I and many houseguests couldn't eat it all. Writer Michael Pollan has talked about having to give away vegetables out of his 10- by 20-foot garden.

Of course, you can't grow the entire panorama of vegetables

in 100 or 200 square feet—personally, I like growing absolutely everything I can—but you can probably grow every vegetable that's really important to you.

Why are beginning gardeners advised to "go small"? Basically, because you are going to have to keep your plot weeded, and that requires another investment called time. Nature abhors a vacuum, especially a vacuum filled with highly enriched soil, and bare neglected earth soon becomes not so bare, but full of fountains of grass and mature weeds that cannot be simply plucked out of the ground, but have to be dug out. So make your garden a size that you can control, or it will be a reproach to you every time you look at it.

You don't have to spend a lot of money to make your garden, but there are some sunk costs in garden-making that it is not wise to deny—particularly fencing against deer, groundhogs, rabbits, and other thieves, if these are likely to be a problem where you garden.

If you live in a city, you may have relatively few competitors for your vegetables and may need no barriers at all. I'd make no such assumptions about any country or suburban yard. I was an experienced gardener by the time I made my current garden in the country, and, even more important, my dog Lulu was an experienced chaser-away of wildlife. For years, we'd gardened in a village yard of 2 acres that backed up to woods and had never needed a fence. Though my neighbor right across the street complained about deer eating her vegetables, we never had any such problems, thanks to Lulu and her big teeth.

Then I made my first garden at a weekend house, on a

15-acre spot on a high road that is reverting to wilderness. I spent all of Memorial Day weekend planting seedlings, as I usually do. I returned the next weekend to find that every single seedling in the brassica family had been chomped off to a mere stem—every broccoli, cabbage, cauliflower, and Brussels sprout in the joint. I bought some more seedlings and planted them again. Gone. I did it a third time, out of sheer stubborn stupidity. Again, the seedlings didn't last from weekend to weekend. My youngest daughter, who was a baby then, loved radishes and cried to see that every little radish plant was shaved off as soon as it appeared. No sooner had a bush bean poked its head out of the ground, but it was eaten. Cilantro? Forget it.

I soon figured out that it was not deer that were causing the problem, since the pole bean vines were only nibbled to about 2 feet up and eventually outgrew predation. Then, I began to see three very fat groundhogs lolling around in the grass near my garden in the early morning. I'd let Lulu out of the house as soon as I woke up, and she'd tear off towards them, barking madly at the fat thieves. But they knew that as part-timers, we were ultimately impotent against them. So they moved off at a tauntingly leisurely pace.

Then I tried a motion-detector sprinkler designed, in theory, to scare off such creatures. It did nothing to keep the groundhogs from nibbling my greens, but my kids found it uproariously enjoyable to turn the sprinkler on while I was working in the garden and blast me with it.

The groundhogs made me murderous, and frankly, that is not

the kind of state a gardener necessarily likes to be in. All I harvested that year were potatoes (too deeply planted for the groundhogs to bother with), tomatoes (too productive for groundhogs to
bite into every last one), arugula (too spicy for groundhog palates),
and pole beans (too tall for groundhogs).

As a beginner, it's crucial to avoid such discouragement, so
fence if you think you need to. Of course, there are investment
choices here, too. My country neighbor managed to stymie his
groundhogs by plunging cheap steel posts into the ground, hanging
chicken wire from them, and securing the bottom with some railroad ties he had lying around. I doubt the entire setup cost more
than $40. On the other hand, you can order a "garden system" from
a company that will come and build you a pest-proof cage in which
to garden for $40,000.

Since I really do appreciate a handsome infrastructure in a
vegetable garden, I'm grateful that in a reckless moment a few
years ago, I spent $3,000 on a cedar picket fence for my 36- by 52-
foot garden. Of course, the fence wasn't truly effective against the
groundhogs until I nailed cage wire to the bottom of it, arduously
digging a trench around the garden perimeter to bury the wire a
foot deep and bend it in another foot. And still my bush beans get
nibbled off in July! I suspect young rabbits here, but this degree of
forced sharing I can put up with.

The wonderful thing about fences is that they can save you
time every year by offering built-in support for tomatoes, which
would otherwise have to be staked or caged, and climbing peas.
You can grow grapes against them, or dahlias and sweet peas, if

you like flowers in the garden. The difficult thing about any serious investment in fencing for beginners is that you'll be making a nearly irrevocable decision about the size of the garden before you have any idea of what you're capable of.

As I said, the standard advice for beginners is, "Go small." However, if you are going to begin your gardening career by erecting a permanent fence, "Go a little bigger" might be the more sensible advice. You want to make sure there is enough space within the posts to suit your eventual ambitions. My own ambitions include staple crops such as potatoes—homegrown potatoes taste so fantastic that I try to grow enough to get my family through the winter—and absurd space-hogging dinosaur breakfasts such as winter squashes, rhubarb, and asparagus.

When I called the fence company, I made sure that my current garden was generous—1,872 square feet, bigger than the vegetable garden I had when I actually lived at the house where I gardened. But now that the permanent crops like the asparagus and rhubarb are mature and my currant and gooseberry bushes are spreading, and my three kids each expect a bed of their own to plant every year, well, it really could be bigger. Too late. The fence is already up.

If you fence a good-sized spot and then find that planting all of it in annual vegetable crops and harvesting and weeding it is too much for you, you can always add a few rows of fruiting bushes or some small fruit trees, with ground-cover perennials and bulbs planted beneath them. Or you could do some really healthy farmer-style soil management with the excess space, letting a different piece of the garden lie fallow under a cover crop every year, which can then be cut down to enrich the soil.

The next great start-up question in the vegetable garden is how you are going to turn what is almost certainly lawn grass now into beautiful garden beds. Ripping up the sod by hand, as I did in my first garden, is cheap in terms of cash, but costs so much in terms of labor and time, especially in heavy soil, that you may well want to lie down and weep after an hour of it.

If you have all the time in the world, you can make a garden just by sheet composting over your sod. You put down layers of newspaper or cardboard, which will block the light to the grass beneath, eventually killing it—and then put layers of organic matter on top—manure, kitchen scraps, leaves, grass clippings, wood chips, straw, whatever you've got. Eventually, these layers will start to break down, the earthworms will start doing their work of pulling this good stuff downwards and mixing it into the earth, and you will wind up with lovely, fluffy soil for your vegetables.

It's inexpensive and easy and kind to the soil, but it will probably take at least a full year to work.

My feeling is that life's too short. I'm a big believer in using gasoline-powered tools exactly once in the life of a vegetable garden: when the garden is being made. Having made my first garden with a lot of violent pick action and agonized shrieking, the next two I've made more calmly, by hiring a guy with a tractor. He'd come, he'd plow, and I'd have a garden. If I were gardening in a small yard that couldn't accommodate a tractor, I'd borrow or rent a rototiller to do the same—chop up the sod and turn over the soil a bit.

Since most vegetables are fast-growing annual crops that transform from a tiny seed to an explosion of leaves and fruits within a few months, they are, naturally, heavy feeders that demand rich soil. So the next step in garden-making is radically improving the soil by getting organic matter into it. What you want for this job is compost, organic matter that has sat in a pile for a while and broken down. Well-composted manure from a horse or dairy or sheep farm is ideal for this purpose, but if there are no local options, even sacks of bagged manure from Wal-Mart flung into your car will answer. Other forms of compost will also do—kitchen compost if you can produce enough of it, composted yard waste or fall leaves, or some lovely combination of the above—a few yards for a small garden, more for a bigger garden, enough to cover the place at least 3 or 4 inches deep.

Some of these soil enrichments can be had for free: I am an inveterate thief of the fall leaves that my silly city neighbors rake to the curb. Some of them are expensive: There is a composting company near me that charges $30 a yard for their stuff plus tax and delivery, which could really break the bank in a garden the size of mine. And some are great bargains: Many cities compost yard waste and will deliver a big truckload for very little. If you hunt around, you are likely to find some professional with a big pile of something good he or she is willing to part with for relatively little money.

My method is simply to rake the pile of organic matter over the plowed garden and turn it into the soil loosely with a shovel. Then I pull out any clumps of grass appearing at the surface, since lawn grasses, as the favored plants of Satan, can regenerate despite being lopped, chopped, and turned upside down, as long as they get a bit of light. Of course, if you are more fastidious than me, you can cart off the sod at an earlier stage—as soon as you've plowed up the garden, or if you are really neat, slice it off the surface before you begin plowing. But I'm always reluctant to remove any form of organic matter from my soil—and to do any unnecessary labor—and prefer to allow the grass to compost in place just by burying it.

The soil can then be raked and the paths marked off. If you like, you can shovel a few inches of beautiful soil out of the paths and onto the planting beds, giving yourself slightly raised beds that will warm up earlier in spring.

The most time-consuming aspect of making a garden for a first time is establishing the territory—marking off boundaries, beds, and paths. You want to leave your planting beds narrow enough that you can easily reach into the middle of them without stepping into them, since your weight will compact the soil, making the beds less root-friendly. Your paths have to be wide enough to allow you to work. While the main axes of my garden are 4 feet wide, more than wide enough for a wheelbarrow, the subsidiary paths I make only wide enough for me to stand in, being stingy about wasting my beautiful soil on them. If I have the time, I measure every path painstakingly with string in the spring. If not, I just eyeball them. I generally mulch them with bark or wood chips to keep down the weeds and offer visual contrast to the rest of the garden. Such painstaking measurement, by the way, is only for appearance's sake. Nature does not demand straight lines in order for food to be grown.

However, if I had the cash, I'd eliminate this annual measuring entirely by investing in a nice stone or brick edging for the garden and stone or brick paths. Fighting back the lawn, which always has colonial ambitions, is *the* epic battle of gardening in much of this suburban nation, so a permanent edge can really save some time. You'll probably still find grass creeping over or under your masonry—and you'll have to dig it out—but you won't have to recut your boundary with an edging spade every year.

Of course, many people save themselves the labor of digging and edging entirely by spending a few hundred dollars on a bit of lumber—whether chunky posts or two by sixes—and slapping it together as a frame for a raised bed. Then they make a garden instantly by pouring imported soil into the frames deep enough to passively smother whatever grass or weeds may be underneath, generally between 8 inches and a foot deep. These beds are usually fairly small, their length dictated by the lumber and their width narrow enough so that the gardener never has to step into them. However, I do know a vegetable garden with four giant raised beds almost as deep as an aboveground swimming pool and staircases that allow the gardener to climb up into these temples to vegetables. That garden makes relatively little horticultural sense to me, but it certainly does look cool.

The advantage of raised beds is that since they are above grade, they warm up more quickly in spring, giving you a jump on the season in places where spring tends to arrive late. They also drain faster, so they are good for soggy spots. People who install raised beds find that they can be planted rather intensively, since they give vegetable roots such a nice deep run of enriched soil. And if the ground beneath them is somehow contaminated—or the only spot you have to garden on is a slab of concrete—you can turn them into deeper plastic-bottomed boxes and bypass the soil entirely.

But raised beds are not ideal everywhere. They make no sense in hot, dry places or places where the soil is already sandy and fast-draining, because whatever water you give them just runs out. Persian gardens often used *sunken* beds, and for a reason.

Now that you've absorbed whatever start-up costs are associated with your garden, the next question is, how do you keep your ongoing expenses down, so the garden turns a profit every year?

My own years of experience in the vegetable garden have turned me into a radical minimalist. It's not just cheaper, it's easier.

I don't really use any tools in my garden except shovel and pitchfork. All kinds of highly specific tools are available for digging, seeding, planting, tilling, and weeding, and different people love different implements. God bless. For me, however, the most irritating waste of time in gardening is searching for some little trowel or dibble I can't find. Shovels are big and cheap and easy to locate, especially because I've got at least four of them hanging around the garden. And the great thing about the point of a shovel is that it always works.

As far as irrigation is concerned, even in my weekend garden, I do just fine with a 10-year-old $70 rain-tower sprinkler and a $68 battery-powered timer.

I don't buy herbicides or insecticides. My one experience with a pest-discouraging powder was with rotenone, an organic pesticide I bought to get rid of Japanese beetles on my roses. The beetles didn't seem to mind, but the roses did, their tender young growth shriveling in dismay. That was it for me and toxins.

Good thing, because they are often shockingly expensive, not to mention an insane hazard to everybody's health. Even the United States Environmental Protection Agency, which permits all kinds of poisons to be sold to gardeners, admits in its childish and insulting "Citizen's Guide to Pest Control and Pesticide Safety" what entirely bad news these products are:

> Anyone can buy a wide variety of "off the shelf" pesticide products to control weeds, unwanted insects, and other pests. . . . Yet, many of the products can be hazardous to people, especially when stored, handled, applied, or disposed of improperly. The results achieved by using chemical pesticides are generally temporary, and repeated treatments may be required. . . . If used incorrectly, home-use pesticide products can be poisonous to humans.

And just because a pesticide is labeled "organic" does not mean it is benign, either.

While the USDA sets the standards that define "organic" in commercial food production—a definition whose value is hotly debated by farmers—to me, growing food organically is not about trading chemicals for their naturally derived equivalents. It's about building beautiful soil using the products of field and farm, not the products of factories. It's about mimicking nature wherever possible. It's about being unintrusive, unwasteful, and unhysterical. And I can't see any reason to be anything but organic in a backyard vegetable garden.

The sad thing is that insecticides, herbicides, and fungicides are almost never necessary in a vegetable garden. Insects, weeds, and diseases are more of a symptom than a cause and tend only to be really troublesome when something is seriously out of balance.

And when they *are* a problem even in a healthy garden, they can usually be managed most efficiently by mechanical means— digging out the weeds, fencing out the groundhogs, yanking out a diseased plant, and picking the Colorado potato beetles off the potato plants as soon as you spot them. As far as threats to my vegetables are concerned, I've yet to meet the insect pest that isn't best dealt with by squeezing.

The potentially most expensive, and certainly most important, form of maintenance in the garden every year is feeding your soil to replenish all the nutrients removed by your vegetables. When I first started gardening, I used to feel obligated to scatter bagged organic fertilizer over my garden. But I've spent years observing what really promotes explosive growth, and it is nothing that comes out of a bag or bottle. Bagged fertilizer? It's the department store night cream of gardening. Ferociously expensive in tiny amounts and does it really *do* anything?

You are far better off saving the cash to buy a truckload of mulch every year, which in my experience is the most efficient way to add fertility and guarantee a bumper crop of everything. Mulch differs from compost in that it is generally coarser and less broken down; it is meant to blanket the soil, not to be dug into it. You can use all kinds of things for this purpose: fall leaves, grass clippings, wood chips from a tree-and-stump-removal guy, straw, the aged bedding of livestock. An annual mulch does many important things for the soil, which I'll talk about later. But it also does many important things for the gardener.

It cuts way down on digging, since you are basically supplying everything your soil needs from the top. It cuts way down on weeding by blocking the sunlight from the weed seeds and preventing them from germinating. It cuts way down on watering because it keeps the soil moisture from evaporating. More than anything else, mulch guarantees that the ratio of work to harvest is absurdly favorable.

The best time to apply this mulch, I find, is in the late fall, after the garden is basically done for the year. That way, the earliest spring weeds never gain a foothold and I am not out there mulching in May while my seedlings languish in their pots, waiting to be planted. Of course, there are years when I can't mulch in fall because one day it's too early to mulch—I'm still pulling too much food out of the garden—and then the next day, it's too late to mulch, because the mulch pile has frozen solid. Then I shrug and mulch in spring.

The great secret about vegetable gardens is that they require less and less time, labor, and money every year as the soil gets richer, as the weed seeds scattered in the soil give up the ghost, as the paths begin to mark themselves, as the gardener develops a method that works. And all those same factors encourage a rising yield. So whatever trouble there is initially in making the garden, it soon turns into a tidy residual business, like appearing on a TV show as a kid and getting checks from it for the rest of your life, or patenting some little scientific discovery that supports you years later, or collecting renewal commissions on the homeowner's insurance you sold in another decade.

That's not to say that I don't work rather furiously in my garden every year at planting time in May and June. It's just that by July, the garden repays that labor so effusively, I feel as if my arms are being filled with unearned gifts.

THREE

Flavor

If You Haven't Grown It, You Haven't Tasted It

One of the best reasons to garden is the fact that homegrown fruits and vegetables just taste so transcendently wonderful.

So incredible that they can turn anybody into a magnificent cook. Even if you are merely a happy amateur in the kitchen, as I am, you may find yourself becoming grandiose as the summer wears on. By mid-September, when harvest season is at its peak, I often mistake myself for Alice Waters, the chef who revolutionized American cooking in the 1970s by emphasizing the fresh and the local at her Berkeley restaurant Chez Panisse.

Alas, when January rolls around and the only homegrown food I have left is a last parsnip in the cellar, I'm once again an enthusiastic but fairly ordinary cook. It's the ingredients, stupid.

Homegrown food tastes better than supermarket conventional produce, better than supermarket organic. It's better even than farmers' market produce, excellent as that usually is, and we'll talk about why in a minute. The truth is, if you haven't grown a vegetable, you may never have really tasted it. Tomatoes and other fruits, with their complex acid/sweet flavors and dramatic transformations on ripening, are classic examples of things supermarkets simply cannot do well. However, even humble staples that taste just fine from the supermarket are an absolute revelation from the garden.

I'm talking about such ignorable items as curly parsley, escarole, potatoes, onions, or dried beans for a chili—perfectly serviceable when purchased from the Price Chopper, but another thing entirely from the garden. It seems as if every year, another unassuming vegetable suddenly turns into a star in my garden and opens up a new frontier in my life as a cook and eater.

Last year's revelation was a green named mâche, very popular in France, that I've planted a few times and ignored. It forms low-growing little rosettes, irritatingly tiny, too small to be worth the bother of cutting and washing, mainly because I never found the flavor particularly interesting. But it has been discreetly seeding itself in my garden in a bed of ever-bearing strawberries, and I haven't been weeding it out.

About a year ago, however, I took notice because as soon as the snow retreated in late March—long before any gardener in my part of the world even thinks about seeding salad greens—there the mâche was, all perky and inviting. Then I popped a plant into my mouth. Allowed to germinate and grow on its own schedule, the leaves were so tender and melting and the flavor so powerful, it was like eating a strong and expensive French perfume, something on the order of Chanel Coco. Amazing.

Let's talk about why food harvested fresh from the garden, still warm from the sun or wet from the rain, offers the greatest possible interest for palate and spirit. It has to do with the nature of plants, of us, and of the food industry in all its desperate attempts to feign naturalness while undercutting nature at every turn.

The important thing to understand about plants is that because they can't run for their lives or do a mating dance, they manufacture chemicals of diabolical subtlety and effectiveness to achieve their goals. They produce chemicals to attract—for example, the chemicals that create the luscious flavor and glorious color of ripe fruit, all designed to draw seed-dispersing animals. On the other hand, some of the chemicals produced by plants are designed to repel hungry herbivores that range from bacteria to groundhogs. Some plants are so subtle that when attacked, they produce a chemical designed to attract the predator of the insect that is eating them.

These chemicals give plants their flavor. One of the theories for why organic foods taste better than the conventionally grown is because organic plants actually face some threats and are forced to mount some tasty defenses, rather than living in a stupid utopia created by pesticides that keeps their flesh bland. Because we adult humans are thrill-seekers, some of the repellent chemicals are part of the enjoyment.

In fact, I sometimes wonder if the difference between my 7-year-old's palate and mine is that her more sensitive palate responds to plants' attempts to seduce—and I appreciate the bite or burn of their attempts to repel. "It's spicy!" she says in an accusatory tone almost every night as dinner is served. Spicy is an all-purpose term that covers far more than hot peppers—raw garlic, horseradish, ginger, and arugula all fit her definition of spicy.

Our perception of flavor is incredibly subtle, and taste is only part of it. Almost all of our senses are involved. The feel of food in our mouths is significant. Appearance, temperature, and memory also contribute. Smell especially is essential to our idea of flavor, which is why it's difficult to appreciate good food with a bad cold. Brain imaging has demonstrated that our perception of flavor is more than the sum of its parts, too. More areas of our brain are activated by the combination of taste and smell that determines flavor than by smell alone plus taste alone.

Taste is, if anything, the blunter part of the system. Taste receptor cells are each tuned to one of five different sensations: sweet, sour, salty, bitter, and savory. In contrast, there are an estimated 350 different kinds of odor receptor cells in the human nose. Each one detects a very specific and limited number of substances. And because individual odors are multifaceted combinations that light up different combinations of receptors, we are able to recognize more than 10,000 different odors.

When it comes to flavor, the apparatus for fussiness is definitely in place!

Our responses to taste appear to be instinctive, since taste sensations offer such very basic survival information—if it's bitter or sour, the plant may well be toxic. If it's sweet, there is a lot of caloric energy there. If it's savory, there is protein to be had. Responses to smell, on the other hand, seem to be learned. My brother Elliot, who lived in Thailand for years, remembers the moment when someone opened up a stall selling coffee in his local market for the tourists. "It was the most heavenly smell," he tells me, "something I'd missed. But to the Thais, the smell was so disgusting that they drove the stand out of there."

The fact that we can learn to love different odors explains the development of the delicious range of different food cultures that is one of the great joys of the modern eater's life. I'm not Thai or Indian or Italian, but boy, do I appreciate a Thai or Indian or Italian take on what good food smells like. A plain steak grilling, widely agreed upon when I was growing up as *the* smell of good food, always bored me to tears. I think I was just killing time as an eater, waiting for ginger and cilantro, fish sauce and basil to enter my life.

The plant chemicals that speak to the sensory apparatus at the top of our noses are volatile compounds—in other words, gases at room or serving temperature. Individual plants can produce hundreds of them, and we may be sensitive only to a small subset, but we may be *very* sensitive to them. The second most important volatile compound in tomatoes, in terms of its contribution to the tomatoes' flavor, we can detect at the level of parts per trillion.

Interestingly enough, almost all of the flavor volatiles in tomatoes are indicators of substances important for our health—either essential nutrients, or antioxidants, anticarcinogens, or antimicrobials (germ-fighters). The same connection between flavor and healthful properties has been established for many vegetables, fruits, and spices. Why do we love something as bitter as the hops in beer? Possibly because the flavor compounds in hops seem to be antimicrobial. When the flavor of a plant is good, it's generally because it *is* good.

While tastes can be manipulated by industrial food manufacturers—every box of factory food has a carefully calibrated mix of sweet, salty, and savory—it's harder to fool the nose with an engineered food. Not that people are not trying. *Fortune* reported in June of 2009 that a company called ScentSational Technologies was working with a baby food manufacturer to incorporate an odor into the jars' seals, so that when parents open them, they can smell "freshness." Someday, ScentSational may figure out how to put the aroma of fresh parsley into a jar of risotto, but until then, you can find me in the garden.

Flavor volatiles are by definition *volatile*—fleeting, ready to evaporate, easily destroyed by industrial processes, dampened down by refrigeration. In fruits, including tomatoes, many of the flavor volatiles are only released at the point of ripeness. As a gardener, you can pick your tomatoes and strawberries when they are *exactly* the right color and texture. Commercial fruit, on the other hand, is often picked hard and unripe because unripe fruit is easier to transport. Then, the plant hormone ethylene, which helps to make ripe fruit soft and sweet, is either sprayed onto the fruit to speed up the process, or carefully controlled to slow it down. How does this fruit, ripened on a distributor's schedule rather than the sun's, taste? It tastes like cardboard.

A few years ago, I just got fed up with supermarket fruit, which was never good enough to eat. I've always grown the herbaceous fruits, strawberries and rhubarb, but I expanded into shrub fruits like currants, gooseberries, blueberries, raspberries, and blackberries, as well as orchard fruits like plums, peaches, sweet and sour cherries, pears, and apricots—plus hardy kiwi vines. So far, the great successes in my two gardens are the currants, peaches, grapes, and raspberries.

Fruit crops do require more patience than vegetables. The ones that grow on woody plants can take a few years to yield much.

And fruit is nature's candy, so when your plants do finally produce ripe fruit, there is likely to be intense competition for it. In the country, I have to net against the birds. In the city of Saratoga Springs, there are other problems.

When I first planted peach trees on my hell strip between the street and the sidewalk, my neighbor Peggy said warningly, "The drunks are going to get those."

"They wouldn't dare," I growled.

People staggering home from the bars at 3:00 in the morning to their rented houses are a feature of summer life in Saratoga Springs, where we have a Victorian-era thoroughbred track, a polo field, a few weeks of the New York City Ballet, and a very high drinking establishment per capita ratio. Saratoga was America's first real resort town, and it's always been glamorously dissipated. In theory, people came to drink the mineral waters from our local springs and improve their health. In actuality, they came to gamble and carouse and find rich husbands, and they gave my fair city a rakish personality that's still a good part of its charm. Unfortunately, tourist season happens to coincide with the ripening of my peaches.

Sure enough, the first year that my trees produced peaches, they disappeared overnight just as they reached ripeness, before I could even taste one. I blamed the squirrels. Then, the next year, one of my neighbors pointed out that squirrels rarely spit neat little piles of peach pits into his empty garbage can. Even in my northern latitudes, these peaches, a variety called 'Garnet Beauty', are worth regretting. They taste like sunshine, like heat, like the all-too-brief bacchanal that is summer in upstate New York. So I've taken to sleeping with one eye open.

With vegetables, unlike with fruit, ripeness is not the issue—
they are often better small and tender. But they are fragile, too.
Food writer Harold McGee's superb reference book, *On Food and
Cooking: The Science and Lore of the Kitchen*, which brings a spirit
of scientific inquiry to the black arts of food preparation, offers this
blanket truth: "Once a vegetable is harvested, it begins to change,
and that change is almost always for the worst."

Cut off from water and nutrients, vegetables continue metabo-
lizing their sugars and accumulating wastes. Some of them convert
that sugar to starch and become bland, and some of them convert
it to lignin and become woody and tough. Asparagus falls into the
latter category. The wisdom among the country gardeners near me
is that asparagus is a crop best cooked a few minutes after harvest.
Fresh asparagus not only has a delicate, sweet flavor, but is ridiculously tender. I can tell the difference if the asparagus I've grown
sits in the refrigerator even overnight. It still tastes good, but the
texture is not the same.

Arugula, my favorite of all salad materials, also never seems to
offer quite the right combination of melting texture and peppery
flavor except when homegrown and eaten soon after it's picked. I
find the same for all leaf lettuces, though the real Alice Waters,
with a famously fine palate, begs to differ. "There's a certain alive-
ness that is part of picking and eating something immediately, that
can be lost in some cases in half a day," she tells me. "But I find
that a salad purchased that morning from the farmers' market still
has that beautiful life about it."

The one exception McGee makes to the fresher, the better
rule among vegetables is "plant parts designed to hibernate, for

example, onions and potatoes." When it comes to potatoes, the excellent McGee—possibly not a gardener?—is just wrong. While any organic potato, I find, is delicious, freshly dug potatoes are exceptionally delicious, just a miracle of lightness and creaminess. The only real improvement I've noticed in stored potatoes occurs, reasonably enough, in my favorite storage potato, a big red variety called 'Sangre' that seems denser after it's been out of the ground for a while.

No, the truly dramatic example of improvement in my root cellar—an improvised space on a crumbling brick staircase between my ill-fitting Victorian cellar door and the Bilco door that leads outside—is the undersung parsnip. This vegetable, which looks like a hearty white carrot, is sugary and creamy, but with a punk edge that no carrot would ever dare attempt.

Finger-sized slices of parsnip roasted in olive oil and salt, with the sugars caramelizing on the outside, is one of the finest dishes known to man. And parsnips, which taste pretty damned good right out of the garden after a few heavy frosts, are even sweeter when they've sat on my cellar stairs for a few months. They just have their moment—in January and February—when they are so delicious, I pity people who don't have Rubbermaid tubs of parsnips buried in wood shavings in their cellars.

It's not just the *quality* of the flavors, either, that argues for a home garden, it's also the *range* of flavors.

People who grow food for money are inevitably constrained by their processes and the tastes of their customers. Commercial growers often rely on just a handful of varieties of fruits and vegetables. These varieties often lack flavor because they have not been bred for flavor. They've been selected for industrial qualities such as uniform appearance, yield, and shipability.

Even the farmers' market farmers near me, much as I love them, can't really afford to prize taste above marketability. The kitchen gardener, on the other hand, has a world of unlimited opportunities spreading out in front of him or her—so many different vegetables, so many different varieties of the same vegetable, which can be dramatically different in appearance and taste.

You can sense the possibilities even in the supermarket, oddly enough. The one that I reluctantly patronize displays a big multi-sided rack of Burpee seeds—Burpee is the great mass-marketer of American seed companies—that offers plenty of amusement even for a jaded old vegetable grower like me: four different kinds of pumpkins, eight different kinds of beans, a dozen pretty sunflowers. Even the Big Box stores near me offer a surprisingly generous selection of seeds, including organic seeds, as well as some of the more romantic heirloom vegetable varieties that are now being rediscovered, such as a watermelon called 'Moon and Stars', which has yellow markings that look like the night sky.

Move beyond the Big Box stores into the seed catalogs, and you will be offered an embarrassment of riches. There are companies that specialize in exotic Indian vegetables or seeds imported from Italy. The beautifully styled and photographed Baker Creek Heirloom Seeds catalog offers 1,400 unusual old varieties of vegetables. The nonprofit Seed Savers Exchange, which is dedicated to preserving heirloom varieties, prints up a yearbook that last year allowed its members to offer 13,571 unique varieties of vegetables to each other.

Why are all these choices meaningful? Because experimentation is both amusing and worthwhile. In fact, it can yield absolute magic. The winemaker's idea of *terroir*—that you can taste the place in the wine and that the same grapes will yield different-tasting wines depending on where they are grown—holds true in the vegetable garden, too. Different varieties are wonderful in different places.

For example, there has been a huge vogue for an heirloom tomato called 'Brandywine' for the last decade or two. 'Brandy-wine' is a big, watery tomato with a thin, unglossy skin and an unbeautiful red-gray color that has a flavor gardeners from Boston to North Carolina rave about. I believe them, but 'Brandywine' is only good from my colder-zone garden in a very hot, dry year. In a more normal year, it is watery and bland. Fortunately, there are other stars in my garden—a tiny currant tomato called 'Matt's Wild Cherry' and an exceptionally sweet red-streaked yellow tomato called 'Pineapple'. I like to roast my 'Pineapples' in a hot oven and then sauté them with ridiculous amounts of garlic, rosemary, and extra virgin olive oil and throw over pasta.

Before I face the firing squad, I will ask for this as my last meal.

I am so attached to 'Pineapple' tomatoes, in fact, as well as to pimiento-type peppers and specific varieties of eggplant that can be impossible to find as seedlings in a nursery, that I do something I really detest to have them: I start their seeds in the house in early April. Tomatoes, eggplants, and peppers require a longer frost-free season than we have in most of the country, so they have to be given a jump on the season and started indoors or in a greenhouse—where their little seedlings will need constant checking for moisture and light and temperature, and one false move will render months of loving care an exercise in futility. Seed starting is babysitting, babysitting somebody else's peevish and ungrateful children. I hate it.

But I have learned a thing or two about it despite myself. And that's that the few sunny windowsills in my dark Victorian house do not offer the right setup for raising sturdy, fast-growing plants—not compared to cheap 48-inch fluorescent tube lights hung from chains in my basement and plugged into a timer that allows them to beam faux sunlight 16 hours a day. I raise the fluorescents as the seedlings grow so the lights are always just a few inches above their heads. Then I kick the seedlings out of the basement into a protected spot in the yard for a week or two before I plant them into the ground, so they can get used to actual sun, rain, and wind.

Of course, I know sophisticated gardeners and cooks who would not dream of going to the trouble of starting seeds. And it is increasingly easy to find a really nice array of interesting vegetable seedlings at both nurseries and farmers' markets. But if you are a true adventurer, seed starting will give you the ultimate freedom to rummage in the storehouses of the world's food cultures. This year, I am growing a red eggplant called 'Cannibal Tomato' that the Baker Creek Heirloom Seeds catalog calls "shockingly bitter" and that reportedly was used for sauce for cannibal meals. I don't expect to see this eggplant at my farmers' market any time soon.

I tend to order a lot of my seed from a cooperative called Fedco located in Waterville, Maine, which sends out a very unslick catalog on newsprint. I like this catalog because it's opinionated and funny and unpretentious and written by true food lovers, and because the things recommended for Maine's short-season climate often work in mine. However, if I lived in the Southwest, I probably wouldn't be taking advice from Fedco. I'd be paying careful attention to the New Mexico–based Seeds of Change.

I must say, however, that climate is not always a limiting factor for vegetables, most of which can be planted, grown, and eaten without ever seeing a single winter. I've been amazed at the success of the things I've ordered from Seeds from Italy, which sells the excellent seeds of Franchi Sementi of Bergamo, Italy. Last summer, the coldest, rainiest, and most non-Mediterranean summer in memory, the one summer squash that really thrived in my garden was called 'Serpent of Sicily'. It seems very Sicilian, that squash's ruthless will to live!

Seeds from Italy allows me to try the favored varieties of a nation of excellent cooks, as well as entirely new vegetables that I've never seen before. This year, I experimented with something called *l'agretto*, a strange starburst of succulent shoots that looks like the kind of green that might be sautéed on Mars. It has a delicious flavor and a texture reminiscent of a Japanese seaweed salad even when cooked.

So how can a beginning gardener who is not yet interested in growing Martian vegetables or cannibal condiments decide what to plant from among thousands and thousands of choices in seed catalogs—or even choose which one of the supermarket's 10 tomato types to try?

There are no wrong choices. At about $2 a pop, a package of vegetable seeds or a flat of seedlings represents the world's most enjoyable shopping opportunity. The risk is minimal, but any random selection has the power to broaden your horizons as a cook and an eater. Ideally, pick what looks good or ask a gardening neighbor what he or she likes to grow. Try a few different varieties of each vegetable, and I promise you, by year two, you will have decidedly firm opinions about what tastes great from your yard.

Since I've had three different-sized gardens over the course of my vegetable career—small, medium, and large—I have developed my own planting priorities, based on the fun of growing, cooking, and eating particular crops. Although flavor preferences are entirely subjective—and my 7-year-old is *extremely* suspicious of mine—the ease of growing a vegetable, its space requirements, and its broad usefulness in the kitchen are less subjective, so let me tell you what I'd plant in gardens of various sizes.

If I had only a 4- by 8-foot raised bed, the choice would be simple: I'd plant the holy triumvirate of basil, tomatoes, and arugula. It's simply not summer without these three things, and they taste incomparably better homegrown rather than bought. Mixed and matched in various combinations with olive oil and vinegar, they will give you a beautiful meal of pasta and a salad over and over and over again.

Plus, arugula and other leaf lettuces are simply the easiest of all crops—throw a handful of seed on top of the soil, wait a few weeks, and cut. In late summer, you may be able to cut the same clump of arugula a few times, but in early summer, arugula tends to send up seed stalks pretty quickly. When leafy plants go to seed, the leaves become attenuated and the stems get woody and the whole thing represents a less appealing eating opportunity. But arugula grows so quickly that it's easy just to yank it out in that case and plant more—or to plan ahead and always have a new crop coming in.

If my space expanded just a little, maybe into a 6- by 10-foot community garden plot, I'd also add some cilantro. It's another do-nothing crop like arugula that requires no more than an occasional scattering of seed. Like arugula, it goes to seed quickly and needs to be replanted several times over the course of the summer. It's also essential if you want to cook Mexican, Indian, or Thai food, which I almost always do. In another corner, I'd shoehorn in some parsley, which doesn't take a lot of room, requires no attention in the garden, and is really good in so many situations, including when you have exactly 12 minutes to prepare dinner and are tired of pesto. The answer then is pasta with sautéed garlic, anchovies, and finely chopped parsley. While most cookbooks will demand Italian or flat-leaf parsley, I find the flavor of curly parsley more intense.

In a few square feet on the north side of the garden, I'd put up some kind of teepee or arch and grow pole beans up it. I know, it seems a little astonishing that anyone would put a mere bean so high on the list of culinary joys, but pole beans have a really rich flavor that bush beans never achieve. I particularly love blanched pole beans in a salad, where their slightly meaty taste and texture offer the perfect contrast to a bath of vinegar. And bean vines are absurdly productive; as long as the beans are picked regularly, the vines will keep growing and producing from midsummer until a frost cuts them down. This is a very forgiving crop, too. If you fail to keep them picked and let the pods get lumpy and overgrown, you can always shell the seeds inside and cook those. They taste great, too.

I can tell you exactly what I'd add if my square footage expanded to 25 by 40, because I used to have a garden of this size. First on the list would be patty pan squashes. While I like zucchinis when picked small, they never have quite the same light, slippery texture of a patty pan. Plus, patty pans have an amusing, flying-saucer shape going for them, and some varieties are the same white-green color as a glow-in-the-dark toy. I slice them thin, put them on a cookie sheet with a generous amount of olive oil and salt, and stick them under the broiler until they are soft and slightly brown. Garnish them with lemon basil, and you have a very fine experience ahead of you indeed.

Close behind on my list of crops would be eggplants, which I like to eat treated exactly the same simple way, except garnished with sweet basil instead. In my northern latitudes, the fat black Italian eggplants never seem to do very well for me. For years, I planted the long Japanese varieties, until I tried a small lavender-streaked white Italian variety called 'Rosa Bianca', which is really tender and delicious from my yard.

I also love red peppers, but I sadly garden where the season is often too short for peppers to ripen to red. I'm nonetheless always trying new varieties of pepper, because once, about 18 years ago, I bought some pimiento-type peppers at the food co-op near me in the country. Generally, red peppers are not good, in my opinion, unless they are roasted and their tough skins removed. But this variety had such a thin skin and such thick, beautiful walls and such a sweet flavor, that simply sliced and sautéed and then thrown over pasta, it would melt and turn the pasta slightly pink. Trust me, I went back to the store to try to find the local truck farmer who'd delivered them so I could learn what variety they were. No luck. Years of experimentation with different seeds in a difficult climate have not yet yielded the same pepper. Whenever I feel discouraged on this score, I remember Winston Churchill's advice, "Never give in. Never, never, never, never—in nothing, great or small, large or petty," and I order a bunch more seeds.

Greens are also very important to me, both for salads and cooking, so a rotating cast of characters among various greens would also have a space in this garden. In some years, there would be escarole, which I love both as a toothsome salad and sautéed, or chard, or mustard greens, or tatsoi, an Asian green which forms pretty flat rosettes of round little leaves. In some years, I'd be in the mood for radicchio. As a heading crop, this can't be too crowded, so I'd leave room for a row. In most years, I'd seed kale in early to midsummer for the fall. Kale has a rich flavor, but even more important, a great, frilly texture. Unlike most greens, kale doesn't collapse into an algaelike mess when cooked. I love a *caldo gallego*–style soup in the late fall: chicken stock with kale, ham, beans, and potatoes or pasta.

Those potatoes would be homegrown, too, even in a relatively small garden. People often think of potatoes as one of those unexciting, space-hogging staple crops best left to farmers, but I find them very efficient. In the same space in which I'd get a few meals' worth of shelling peas—which are all hat and no cowboy, all vine and pod and precious little pea—I can harvest 50 pounds of potatoes. And they taste so great out of the garden. Commercially grown potatoes are inedible, in my opinion. They are drenched in pesticides during the growing process, which may explain their weird, watery texture and nasty flavor.

Potatoes are so forgiving as a crop that you can plant them in April or in August in my part of the world, or at any point in between. I usually do both. While some of them take 100 days to mature, other varieties take just 60. I find them the perfect replacement crop in midsummer for peas, spinach, strawberry plants, and other stuff that poops out early. They are also not fussy about when you harvest them. In fact, if you are impatient, you can start stealing potatoes from the edges of the plant early just by feeling around in the soil. The mass of them are ready to be harvested after the plants have bloomed and begun to yellow and wither, but you can still let the potatoes sit in the ground for a while if you're busy. You just have to make sure you harvest them before the mice get them or they freeze.

Harvesting them is fun. I fork up the plant, and my kids love spotting them and picking them out of the soil. Plus, my children behave as if I've just served them ice cream whenever I put potatoes on the table. They are crazy about potato leek soup, so I would plant leeks, too, which don't take up a lot of room, for their buttery flavor.

Many of the brassica—the family that includes cabbage, broccoli, and Brussels sprouts—grow into big, handsome plants that demand some room, so I probably wouldn't be growing a lot of cabbages and broccolis in a garden with limited square footage. I'd save the space for Brussels sprouts because they are so sweet when roasted after a frost—and because they are so tough about surviving freezing and thawing and freezing that they are the very last thing that can be harvested out of the winter garden. I've been out in the garden on Christmas Day with a pick, chopping down a frozen plant. I've also had plants survive intact under the snow over the winter and harvested the sprouts in March.

Now that I have 1,872 square feet in which to garden, my culinary horizons have expanded. I have room not just for a row of broccoli, as well as cabbages for coleslaw and sauerkraut, but also for one or two of the favored winter squashes and pumpkins. These are field crops that send out enormous vines of enormous leaves that often yield only a couple of fruits apiece in a good year. While my youngest daughter's jack-o'-lantern pumpkins grow in the meadow behind the garden, I make room inside my fence for a beautiful blue pumpkin called 'Jarrahdale', because pumpkin pie made with fresh pumpkin is so light and delicious, and because it stores so easily over the winter, even in a heated room.

My garden is big enough, in fact, that I can grow crops most sensible people would consider more trouble than they are worth. For example, for the last few years, I've given one of my cast-iron arches to an heirloom shelling bean named 'True Red Cranberry' that is exceptionally pretty, with a shiny maroon color and an interesting bullet shape.

You can order organic dried beans online for $2 or $3 a pound—but not this variety. I let the beans dry on the vine in the fall. Then I yank the vine off the arch and try to bribe my kids to take on the job of shelling them. This is so boring that even a kid desperate for a new computer game may refuse. I amuse myself sometimes by reading the threshing recommendations on the back of seed packages—pillowcases swirled over heads, window screens, and fans often figure prominently—before going back to the no-tech method of splitting the pods with a fingernail and dropping the contents into a bucket.

Why would anyone bother? The chili. I love chili, and 'True Red Cranberry' beans cook up creamy without disintegrating, and they just have a richer flavor than any other red bean I've ever tasted.

Another of the great joys of having a big garden is being able to justify delicious but unreliable crops like Charentais melons, a perfumy little cantaloupe-type melon that would prefer to grow in France—wouldn't we all—but that will occasionally ripen before winter in upstate New York. Another joy is being able to accommodate everybody's tastes. I plant snow peas for my son Milo and shelling peas for my daughter Grace. I plant celeriac, an ugly but delicate-tasting root vegetable, for the wife of the alpaca farmer who lends his wonderful manure to my operation. I plant red cabbages for my mother, who makes a terrific dish of cabbage with bacon, vinegar, and apples. I plant strawberries for Jeff.

I like having a big garden because I can justify a crop like turnips that nobody but me likes. Even a sophisticated eater like my husband finds them nasty, but glazed or just boiled and tossed in butter and chopped parsley, I find them nasty/sublime. Just like carrots, radishes, beets, and parsnips, turnips require the huge discipline and excruciating boredom of thinning out the crowded plants while small. Otherwise, the root will not bulk up. But there is always a silver lining even with grossly mismanaged turnips: turnip greens! Sautéed with bacon and shallots and turned over pasta, they are spectacular.

You name it—watercress, flat Italian onions, edamame, collards, tomatillos, German beer radishes, Malabar spinach—it's probably in my garden as we speak. I have gooseberry bushes there, too, just because I have such fond memories of the delicious gooseberry pie they made at an English tea shop in Los Angeles owned by three delightful Oxford-educated Iranian men, where I waited tables in my youth.

If my planting scheme seems panoramic, it is. I want to grow everything, the fruits and vegetables that I love, as well as the ones that I just don't. I'm a gardener who cooks, rather than the other way around. I have to confess, I simply get a kick out of seeing how different things grow.

The cooks I know who garden are far more focused about their planting choices than I am. They grow just those crops that are most rewarding in the kitchen.

Alice Waters, for example, who is probably more responsible than anybody for the gourmet style of local farming that America now enjoys—and who clearly has access to the finest of farmed produce—nonetheless has always had a small garden in her backyard, which served as the first salad garden for Chez Panisse.

"There are only trees and herbs and salad in my garden," she explains. "I'm not there all the time. But I'm thinking about how things progress through the year. I'm constantly replanting salad. I have a big old bush of rosemary. Thyme and marjoram. Lemons from the lemon tree, a bay tree, a persimmon tree."

While she offers a number of lovely spiritual and aesthetic reasons for gardening, the first reason is practical. "I just can't rely on having the time to run to the restaurant or to the farmers' market. It's so gratifying to go out back and pick some herbs. If you have a little larder with some grains, it's so easy to make something delicious. I plant rocket throughout the year," she says, using the French- rather than Italian-derived name for arugula, "and I'll make rocket pesto."

The garden, in other words, allows a busy woman to eat fast food that's actually wonderful.

The most superlative cook among my circle of friends is my country neighbor Martha Culliton. Martha is not a public figure like Alice Waters, nor is she running a restaurant these days, but she is similarly practical about her garden. "While I'm interested in the texture and beauty of plants," Martha explains, "I came to the realization that I'm not much of a gardener. What I am is a farmer on a tiny, tiny scale."

It was actually Martha's exquisite vegetables that led to her career as a chef. Some 25 or so years ago, she'd invited the founders of a restaurant called Dacha to dinner. By all reports, Dacha was one of the best restaurants ever to grace upstate New York. Martha served something unusual from her garden—she remembers "radish-sized Japanese turnips"—and next thing you know, Dacha was buying vegetables from her.

Then, one summer, Dacha hired a sous-chef from New York

City. "The guy took one look around at his bucolic surroundings," chuckles Martha, "and realized he was probably not going to get laid for the next 6 months. He went immediately back to where he came from."

So Martha, already an accomplished home cook in her twenties, was offered the job. She rose to chef, but workdays that lasted from 9:00 a.m. to 1:00 a.m. eventually convinced her that an advanced degree in art history was called for. Now you have to be her friend to taste her food.

Ask Martha what she gets out of her garden that she couldn't just as well get out of the Salem, New York, farmers' market and she will hand you a 'Triumph de Farcy' green bean the size of a nail. "This is what I can't get at the farmers' market—green beans this size. A farmer would have to let them grow on to get more bang for the buck. And the difference in quality is astonishing. I can harvest things at exactly the moment I want. The cucumbers can be cornichon-sized; the zucchinis can have their blossoms still attached."

She pulls a jar out of her pantry and twists off the top. "If I want to make kosher pickles, not only do I have a crop of the sweetest, juiciest cucumbers and a raft of dill gone to seed, even more important, I have the green seeds of coriander—not dried, not the leaf." Indeed, the green coriander balls at the end of an umbrella-shaped stalk add a wonderful texture and flavor to those pickles.

"Many old pickle recipes use grape leaves to keep things crisp," Martha continues. "Maybe you could find grape leaves at some market in the world . . . but not here. But I have grapes in the garden."

Martha continues to pull jars out of her pantry—homemade paprika, more pickles—while naming varieties of vegetables that the local farmers don't plant: a winter squash named 'Delicata', 'Cajun Jewel' okra, my beloved 'Jarrahdale' pumpkin and one I haven't tried called 'Winter Luxury', a crisp and mild Middle Eastern cucumber named 'Zagross', a Spanish pepper called 'Pedrone' that Martha advises "blasting in a hot pan with really good olive oil and serving with sea salt as tapas."

Why does Martha garden? "It gives me a fantastic condition of control over the varieties, harvesting, and storage." In other words, she's too serious about the food she cooks *not* to garden. Her garden doesn't have flowers the way mine does or a pretty infrastructure. She doesn't grow a hundred different kinds of vegetables. Instead, she does particular things in great volume in order to process them. She won't bother to plant things that she finds are just as good from the farmers' market. She's not constantly doing science experiments in the garden like I am. She's not gardening for the sake of gardening; it's a means to an end.

I think gardening like a cook is a fantastic formula for any beginner. Plant what you are most interested in eating and cooking. If you are busy, focus on what will give you the most pleasure for the least amount of time. Garden so you can make pesto in 10 minutes or risotto, which magnifies the flavors of fresh vegetables beautifully, in 25. Leave duty to the supermarkets. If you don't like Brussels sprouts, don't bother. Grow kale instead. Grow what will make you happy.

But I hope you'll leave at least a little space in the garden for exploration, because the endless frontier is the thing that makes both cooking and gardening so satisfying. And it *is* endless. According to Harold McGee, we cultivate merely 2,000 species of plants today, when an estimated 300,000 are edible.

I hope you'll be open-minded, even within the category of known food. Plant a vegetable that bores you, and you may well find yourself loving it, once it's homegrown. Order from one of the terrific seed catalogs that offer the weird and wonderful, and you may discover something entirely new. You may even have the satisfaction of serving an astonished audience something they have never tasted before—tatsoi, fuzzy melon, celeriac, purslane, parsnips.

That's the kind of thing that turns cooks into gardeners.

FOUR

Health

Eternal Youth's Not in a Fountain, But in a Garden

My town of Saratoga Springs has a very glamorous new YMCA building, with a room the size of a football field filled with whining plug-in exercise machines and panting people of all ages and degrees of attractiveness working up a sweat on them. This room is very popular, even within my own family. And I have used it, on occasion, in the dead of winter when one of my children was at a swim lesson and I had precisely 41 minutes to kill.

But mainly, I look at those health and beauty seekers on their various frantic contraptions and consider them total fools, because they could all be gardening instead. They are not out in the fresh air and sun; they are indoors under fluorescent lights and surrounded by a level of climate control that is clearly utterly decadent at a moment of climate change. They are not enjoying a private moment with the plants and birds; they are sweating in public in a way that embarrasses me. They are adding nothing to the world and, I'd venture to say, enjoying nothing other than the animal satisfaction of moving their bodies, a satisfaction that has to be considerably blunted by the unpleasant artificiality of their surroundings. And while there is no question that the benefits of exercise go far beyond the superficial, these treadmill and rowing machine patrons are not getting beautiful from the inside out, as well as the outside in, by eating pole beans off a vine.

Is a vegetable garden better for your health than a gym membership? As far as I know, no scientist has yet organized a controlled experiment to find an answer to this question. But the answer is clear to me. A vegetable garden is a profoundly healthy thing, and not just for the gardener, but for all the other members of the family as well.

The most basic health effect of a vegetable garden could not be more obvious. So many of the medical problems of modern life seem to be diet-determined, including obesity, high blood pressure, diabetes, heart disease, and some cancers. A diet richer in fruits and vegetables can help prevent or reverse these conditions. If these foods are right there in the backyard, brilliant-tasting, available in luxurious quantities for plucking on a whim, you are clearly much more likely to make them part of your diet.

Simply consuming *more* fruits and vegetables is clearly a good thing. And the ones you consume from your own garden are provably better for your health in some ways. First of all, they are unlikely to make you sick. Unless you or your neighbors regularly bomb the lawns around your garden with chemicals or they are already in your water supply, pesticide residues are probably not much of a worry.

And bacterial contamination from polluted water or inept handling is probably not a worry, either. While cooking kills most pathogens, we eat many vegetables and most fruits raw, and there have been a number of horror stories of food-borne illnesses caused by commercially farmed raw fruits and vegetables in recent years. These include bagged spinach contaminated with the sometimes lethal *E. coli* O157:H7, and jalapeño peppers and possibly tomatoes contaminated with salmonella. Organic foods have not been exempt, either.

Salmonella and *E. coli* are both carried in the digestive tracts of animals and people and can contaminate vegetables if they wind up in the water supply. Since your home garden is unlikely to be right next to a poultry or hog farm or dairy or cattle feedlot, and you can avoid fresh manure in it—we'll talk about this in the next chapter—and you are unlikely to use your garden as a substitute for indoor plumbing, you probably do not have to worry much about the safety of your own raw fruits and vegetables. I'd never recommend this for anyone else, but I don't fret much in my own garden about pulling a carrot out of my soil, wiping it off on my pants, and eating it right in place.

Are the foods you grow also healthier because they are more nutritious? I take it as a matter of faith. I'm a food person. They taste better, so they must be better for you.

But if you want scientific proof, we'll have to use studies of organic produce as a proxy for homegrown. It's been difficult to prove once and for all that organic fruits and vegetables are nutritionally superior to conventionally grown for the same reason that all blanket statements about gardening are suspect: Conditions always vary. The nutrient quantities in food can change depending on the vegetable variety, the moment at which they are harvested, the amount of water in their flesh, as well as the many atmospheric and soil conditions that make gardening in one place different from gardening 30 feet up the road and gardening in one season different from the next. It's hard, if not impossible, to control for all of the variables.

As a result, the party line is that organic vegetables have not yet been proven to be overwhelmingly healthier. The USDA's Alternative Farming Systems Information Center puts it this way: "Some scientific papers conclude that certain organic foods are more nutritious than conventional ones; however, other studies find no difference or that conventional foods are, in some cases, more healthful. When examined carefully, though, very few of the studies, regardless of their conclusions, meet basic criteria for good science."

However, The Organic Center published a review of the scientific literature in March of 2008 that argues that the nutritional superiority of organic foods *has* been established. From 97 studies, the review's authors found 236 matched pairs that met their standards, side-by-side comparisons of the same crop grown organically and conventionally. For 11 essential nutrients, the organic samples averaged a 25 percent advantage over conventionally grown, including total antioxidant capacity.

Of course, side-by-side comparisons are not the only way to look at the question of which vegetables are better for you. You can also look at what's happened over time. As farming has become more industrial since the first half of the 20th century, the nutrient value of fruits and vegetables has declined. When Popeye was eating it, spinach clearly meant something! Does it today?

A team led by Dr. Donald R. Davis at the University of Texas compared the USDA food composition data for 43 garden crops in 1950 and 1999. In the products of modern farming, they found significant declines in six nutrients, including protein, calcium, phosphorus, riboflavin, ascorbic acid, and iron. This study hypothesizes that the reason for the decline stems from "decades of selecting food crops for high yield, resulting in inadvertent trade-offs of reduced nutrient concentrations." Over the years, commercial crop varieties have been bred for their friendliness to industrial methods and easy marketing—generally because they produce heavily, grow quickly, are pest-resistant, ship well, and have an attractive, uniform appearance.

Dr. Davis and company explain, "It is well accepted in agricultural research that selecting for one resource-using function may take resources away from other resource-using functions." In other words, beauty requires some effort. Ask any movie star. It takes work for a plant to produce large quantities of gorgeous, big, indestructible, perfectly regular fruits and vegetables, and there may be little energy left over for nutrient production.

So the genetics of commercial crops may make them less nutritious. Other people have noted an environmental "dilution effect"—that when you achieve rapid growth and high yields by applying lots of fertilizer, as happens in conventional farming, the nutrient concentration diminishes. In addition, conventionally farmed soil is simply stupider soil, since many of the creatures underground that help to create beautiful garden soil can't survive or thrive with the overapplication of chemical fertilizers and pesticides. And that, too, may influence the quality of what we eat.

Dr. Jerry Glover, an agro-ecologist at The Land Institute, has been part of a 10-year apple production study that has demonstrated that organic fruits are sweeter, firmer, and better for storage than those grown conventionally or in orchards that integrate conventional and organic practices. The study also looked at the life in the soil, using tiny worms called nematodes as indicators, and found a correlation between the diversity of nematode species in organic soils and better fruits.

We'll talk more in the next chapter about why a soil ecosystem that is full of life is so important to your crops. Suffice it to say here that plants need nitrogen, which is often the limiting factor in their growth. It is either supplied naturally by soil microbes or it is supplied by chemical fertilizers—and the choice seems to affect the quality of what we eat.

"The story you'll hear from folks opposed to organic practices," says Dr. Glover, "is that plants don't care where the nitrogen comes from. Well, it may be true that the plants take up the same form of nitrogen, but the pathways through which the nutrients are transformed are different. Though the mechanisms are not yet clear, we know there are distinct differences in how a plant grows, tastes, and stores in improved soil conditions."

Ultimately, it doesn't really matter whether genetics or environment is the key factor in the nutritional value of the vegetables and fruits that we eat. As a gardener, you easily control *both* genetics and environment. You can plant heirloom varieties rather than more modern high-yield varieties—or plant brand-new varieties bred for qualities other than yield—and accept that your broccoli's head may be slightly smaller than your own. And you can grow them without the use of chemical fertilizers to pump up the plant artificially, and manage your soil for maximum biodiversity. You can have your cake and your antioxidants, too.

Even if you do grow this better-quality food, will its quality make any difference in your long-term health? That's not been proven. Animal studies, however, show that rabbits, rats, and hens fed organically are healthier and better reproducers. They also show that hens, rabbits, mice, and rats, when given a choice, actually prefer organic food. Smarter than many of the people I know, for sure.

But gardening is not just good for your health because of what you ingest. It's also wonderful exercise for your body. In fact, it sometimes occurs to me that I love to garden mainly because I love the exercise. I find digging exhilarating, and in those months when the ground is frozen as hard as cast iron, I miss my shovel terribly and feel cranky and sluggish without it.

The American College of Sports Medicine and the American Heart Association, which together publish recommendations for physical activity, like my shovel. They say that healthy adults need moderate-intensity aerobic activity at least 30 minutes 5 days a week, or vigorous-intensity aerobic activity for 20 minutes 3 days a week. They point out that moderate- or vigorous-intensity activities "performed as part of daily life" even in 10-minute increments count towards this goal, and use "gardening with shovel" as an example. Non-gardeners tend not to imagine that gardening has any aerobic element whatsoever. But it does, especially if you are like me and always in a tearing rush to fulfill absurd ambitions in the time allotted by a short growing season.

Of course, 150 minutes of moderate-intensity aerobic activity a week is just a minimum. More is better. Dr. Candice Shoemaker of Kansas State University, who studies the effects of gardening on aging, points out what is so diabolically effective about gardening as aerobic exercise: "The neat thing about gardening is that 30 minutes fly by, an hour flies by. I can be outside working in the yard for 3 hours before I look up."

If everybody leaves me alone on a weekend, I can happily be outside working for 8 straight hours. Outside is *nice*. But after half an hour on a treadmill in a gym, I fear for my sanity. Having reached an age where if I don't exercise, I am instantly fat, I actually run in the winter when I can't garden—in poky fashion, outside, where I can admire the pretty Victorian architecture of Saratoga Springs. But I find that even when I am serious and the weather is good and I run 5 miles three or four times a week, running is not as effective at keeping excess weight off as working in the garden. Every year in April, as soon as I start mulching, an arduous but invigorating and enjoyable chore involving shovel or pitchfork and wheelbarrow, I lose 5 pounds.

A group led by Dr. Barbara Ainsworth of the University of South Carolina has created a "Compendium of Physical Activities" that records the metabolic equivalents (METs) or energy costs of various activities. A single MET is the energy used at rest. The laborious stuff in gardening—digging, shoveling compost, using a wheelbarrow—all comes in around 5 METs. Running at my pace of 6 miles an hour is 10 METs—clearly a more intense form of exercise, though, I don't know, Dr. Ainsworth and company have never seen *me* with a wheelbarrow. But what gardening lacks in intensity compared to running, it more than makes up for in do-ability over a long period of time.

As a rough rule of thumb, to translate METs into calories expended, multiply half your body weight in pounds times METs. For a 120-pound person, digging represents 300 calories an hour. For a 200-pound person, it would be 500 calories an hour. For a full afternoon of digging, a lot of calories burned.

Of course, exercise is not just about calorie-burning. It's about making sure your body works without causing you too much trouble. When I was in my early thirties, I already had something that qualified as an ache and a pain. My rotator cuff was constantly sore, a ragged kind of pain that sometimes made me quite miserable lying on my side in bed at night. No, I was never a pitcher in the Major Leagues, never injured by throwing too many 90-mile-an-hour fastballs. I was just a ne'er-do-well who wasted her post-college years waiting tables when she should have been more gainfully employed. And I'd clearly lifted one tray full of margaritas too many on my right side.

However, as soon as I picked up a shovel, whatever weakness there was in my back and shoulder disappeared. Now, I'm 50 and my friends are starting to complain about their knees and backs. Me, I feel just as great as I felt at 21. Better even. I'm fitter.

The American College of Sports Medicine has more to say on this subject: "Ideally, exercise for healthy aging should include a combination of aerobic, strengthening, and flexibility exercises."

Gardening wins on all counts. There's proof, for example, that gardening keeps you strong. In 2002, a group led by Dr. Lori Turner, who is now the chair of the health sciences department at the University of Alabama, took a look at 3,310 women age 50 and older whose health information had been surveyed by the National Center for Health Statistics to see which physical activities seemed to influence bone density. "When we saw the results for the first time," Dr. Turner laughs, "we were all, '*What?!*'"

There were only two activities that appeared to contribute significantly to bone mass in this group: the obvious one, weight training, since bone forms in response to the stress of supporting weight, and the one that threw the researchers for a loop, yard work. "We all had the same misconception about gardening," says Dr. Turner. "We never thought of it as rigorous. We thought of it as *dainty*."

That is an opinion that could only be held by a non-gardener. Dr. Turner, however, became a gardener for the first time during the course of the study. "I bought my first house and had my first experience doing some landscaping. I was fairly fit; I worked out at the gym," she laughs ruefully. "But after spending a day gardening, I'd go to bed and just say, 'Oh my word, *that* was exercise!'"

Gardening probably requires more weight-bearing activity than any other hobby short of building stone walls. "There's lifting, squatting, pushing, pulling, bending. If you live where the ground is hard, digging can be really intense," Dr. Turner adds. Garden long enough and you will find yourself lifting balled and burlapped shrubs casually and pushing wheelbarrows filled to the brim with wet compost over hill and dale. Garden long enough, in fact, and you will laugh when the young guy in the wine store offers to carry that case of wine to your car.

If you are younger than 30, all this strength-training through gardening can help you form stronger bones for life. If you are older than 30, you are already losing bone mass, and gardening can help to keep your bones intact and minimize the risk of extreme frailty that is osteoporosis, one of the most common diseases of aging. Dr. Turner speculates that it's not just the fact that gardening is weight-bearing that makes it so valuable for bone density: It's also the fact that people like it, and are motivated to do it regularly in a way that they are not necessarily motivated to lift barbells.

"The fact that yard work requires being outdoors may also be related to bone health," she adds. "You're going to get some vitamin D from the sun, which enhances calcium absorption, which is crucial for bones."

Vitamin D, which is almost impossible to obtain in sufficient quantities from diet alone—we need either the sun on our skin to synthesize it or to take supplements—not only protects against bone disorders, it also seems to protect against an array of chronic diseases, including heart disease, cancer, diabetes, and multiple sclerosis. Yet various studies have found that somewhere between a third and half of all Americans are not getting enough, thanks to the diligent use of sunscreen and a life focused on the great indoors. Just half an hour of unprotected sun exposure a few times a week— even on your arms and legs if you dare not expose your face—is more than enough to prevent vitamin D deficiency. If you have a vegetable garden, getting this sun is likely to be a piece of cake.

Dr. Turner points out that when you gain strength by gardening, you gain more than strong bones. "You'll develop more muscle mass and have a more attractive physique, which is important! You can eat more—lean muscle mass burns more calories. It will influence the overall function of your body's metabolism. Insulin responds better to lean muscle mass, so you'll be preventing diabetes. Plus, you'll be more confident and independent. Instead of asking for help, you can just say, 'Watch me do it.'"

I think independence is great, too. As a relatively small person, I have some limits, but you'd be surprised to look at me to learn how far out those limits are. And I seem to keep getting stronger. Last year, I laid a path using 2-foot by 2-foot pieces of bluestone 2 inches thick. This year, I managed to set the enormous, heavy, Chinese earthenware dragon pot I bought in a New Jersey antiques warehouse for $75 into the garden by myself. Frankly, I'd far rather do the heavy lifting than engage in the psychological warfare required to get the less interested members of the household to do my bidding. Now *that's* exhausting.

But gardening doesn't just make you strong and fit; it also makes you quick and flexible. To dig, plant, weed, water, and pick, you'll be up, down, bending, stretching, reaching, lunging, and balancing on one toe in order not to step on a seedling all day long. Gardening activities like shoveling and wheeling your barrow use many muscle groups simultaneously, arms as well as legs. To begin gardening in spring after a long winter is to feel sore all over. Your whole body is exercised.

Dr. Shoemaker puts her finger on another reason that gardening is so effective as an exercise program—because the punishment for not doing it is shaming yourself in front of the neighbors. "You can ignore a road that's saying, 'Come and walk.' But a plant will tell you if it's not been watered. If you neglect the garden, you'll see the weeds creep in."

She also likes the instant gratification gardening offers. "Other physical activities, you have to do regularly long enough to feel good. It takes a while to get there. But with gardening, there is an instant, tangible result—beautiful flowers, beautiful food. I'm an active flower gardener. When I'm done cleaning out a flower bed, I'll sit back and admire my work. If I've done 30 minutes on a treadmill, I don't stand there admiring the treadmill."

That's right. And when I'm done exercising, I don't stand there admiring the mirror, either. The truth is, for all gardening will do for your body, at a certain point in life, most of us are willing to cede the job of looking gorgeous to the next generation, and self-beautification starts to seem less interesting than beautifying the world. I've reached the stage of life where I'm mainly interested in making things and only willing to expend huge amounts of energy if there is something concrete to point to at the end. And I am clearly not alone. Dr. Turner says that when the first news reports about her study came out, she got many e-mails from her friends thanking her for justifying all the time they spent in the yard—and releasing them from their obligation to spend hours in the gym.

Gardening is one of the few workouts besides carpentry or masonry or sculpting monuments that allows you to build something while you exercise. And what you are building is generally so absurdly beautiful, it is guaranteed to lift your spirits at the end of your labors.

What will a lifetime of gardening do for you? The anecdotal proof abounds. Just take a look around at any serious gardeners among your neighbors who are a few decades older than you. They are likely to look more like Clint Eastwood than your average AARP member. The first real gardeners I ever met, my friends

Bob Nunnelly and Gerald Coble, painters who have made the most beautiful vegetable garden I know, are now around 80 and are as handsome as can be and still pushing into new frontiers in their artwork.

Eleanor Perényi's 1981 collection of essays, *Green Thoughts*, one of the two or three most delightful books ever written about gardening, includes a piece titled "Longevity" that catalogs the unusually long life spans of famous gardeners throughout history, starting with the ancient Greeks and Romans. Perényi concludes, "I like to think of these statistics when I am down on my hands and knees grubbing, while my non-gardening friends are out on the tennis court or jogging past the fence. The athletic tend to look down on gardening—until they try it. Then I am amused to hear their moans and groans. . . . I figure my chances for a long life are at least as good as the average athlete's, and maybe a lot better."

Indeed, Perényi lived to the very gardener-like age of 91, despite appearing with both cigarette and cocktail in hand in her dust-jacket photo on the original edition of *Green Thoughts*.

The gardeners in my own family support Perényi's argument. My grandmother was using a hoe until the age of 89. My husband's grandmother, who owned a piece of magical California bottomland where everything grew at five times the normal rate, was out there planting her tomatoes into her early nineties.

Good food and hard physical labor probably do much to explain the longevity of gardeners, but I have another theory for why gardeners get to be so very old: They can't throw in the towel until they've seen the results of their hard work. In fall, there's always next spring, when the ground they've prepared will begin to

FIVE

The Soil

Why Dirt Isn't Dirty

Contact with good garden soil is just amazingly pleasant. Every time you stick a trowel into it to plant a seedling, a whiff of something fresh and wet and clean comes off of it. Good soil has a beautiful black-brown color and wonderful crumbly texture that gardeners often compare to chocolate cake. It yields in the nicest way when you pull an orange carrot or red radish or lavender turnip out of it. It feels good on your hands, and it feels good on your heels.

But in America, only the gardeners know that soil is delightful—because we have a huge national prejudice against dirt.

We don't like dirt on our persons, clearly. Facial tissue, toothpaste in a tube, dental floss, deodorant soap—these are all American inventions. We are the world's most famous showerers. We take personal cleanliness and the need to spend many hours grooming ourselves so seriously, in fact, that we increasingly build our houses as if one bathroom per person is a reasonable standard. And we don't like dirt in our immediate environment, either—just check out the magnificent array of scrubbing and sprout vegetables and flowers again. In spring, there is always next fall, when they can finally harvest those vegetables whose seedlings they babied for months on a windowsill. So gardeners always have to stick around for another season or two just to see the fruits of their labors, and leaving town is simply not an option.

Take up gardening and you, too, may find it impossible to die.

scouring products in any supermarket. We can buy specific tools for each and every household surface: toilet cleanser, shower cleanser, floor cleanser, oven cleanser, stovetop cleanser, window cleanser, countertop cleanser, even air cleanser. We are upping the ante all the time, too, adding antibacterials to our hand and dish soaps, and now "swiffering" our floors with disposable cloths rather than a broom and mop, which might harbor something residual simply by being reusable. (Of course, in the larger world, we Americans are considerably more slovenly, ranking an embarrassing 61st on Yale and Columbia's international Environmental Performance Index, which rates countries on factors that range from greenhouse gas emissions to environmental impacts on public health.)

I grew up in a household that was virulently anti-dirt, anti-disorder, and only barely tolerant of the savage wolf pack that my brothers and I represented as children. My mother will announce, "I've always been a very clean person," as if her fastidiousness were among the highest of human virtues.

Nonetheless, her desire for order and newness and gleaming cleanliness is honestly won. As I mentioned earlier, she grew up on a charmless pig farm with no screens on the house windows and fly paper curling down from the ceiling like the party decorations in hell. My mother's dislike of dirt also does not mean that she is not a true nature lover. In the midst of a crowded New Jersey suburb, she lives in a very unusual spot, at the edge of an old celery farm that's been turned into a 100-acre nature preserve, with a view of a marshy lake and wonderful trails for bird-watching. She walks 3 or 4 miles there every day.

More typical is my mother's neighbor, a smart, attractive career woman in her early thirties with three small children. They live in a luxurious condo without much of a yard to play in. I ran into her one morning and remarked, "It must be wonderful for your kids, living next to the celery farm, where they have so much room to run around."

She looked at me as if I'd suggested something truly revolting. "We don't go down there. It's *muddy*."

Apparently, mud on everybody's boots represents such a tailspin that even the thrill of observing a great blue heron in flight couldn't begin to pull this woman out of it. This is a very strange attitude, but it is probably the dominant attitude in our culture: Dirt is disgusting. It's dangerous to the carpets. It's dangerous to the kids. It's dangerous, period, at levels too profound even to explain, so dangerous as to be paralyzing—which is why there are a number of self-help gurus online willing to take a credit card number and sell you a workbook and an audio file to help you overcome your dirt phobia—or, if you have thousands to spend, to set you up with a "practitioner" to help you vanquish your fear of mud.

When it comes to Mother Nature, we Americans don't make much of a distinction any more between the beautiful, fruitful earth and decay that really *is* foul. I'll talk in a moment about why the distinction is important and why soil is best thought of as a mechanism to convert the latter into the former. But first, I want to consider the sources of our prejudice against the good earth.

Admittedly, the question of what's germ-ridden and what's merely dirty is not simple. And even a very blunt preference for cleanliness was once a huge step forward. We Americans didn't start off our history as the cleanest people on earth. We spent 2 centuries being notably repulsive in our lack of hygiene. In *Chasing Dirt: The American Pursuit of Cleanliness*, historian Suellen Hoy records the disgusted reactions of 18th- and 19th-century European travelers at the dirtiness of American people, including that of one Englishman who found Midwesterners "filthy, bordering on beastly." Americans didn't think much about washing themselves, their clothes, their bedsheets and their houses, possibly because they couldn't. The only water source for a farm might be far distant from the house. And most cities didn't have adequate public water—or sewage systems—until the late 19th century.

Americans began paying more attention to cleanliness because of two great historical forces. First, there was the increasing urbanization spurred by the Industrial Revolution—and the epidemics of infectious diseases like cholera, typhoid fever, typhus, and yellow fever that swept through crowded cities with few provisions for sanitation. Finding a way to dispose of sewage became a matter of survival.

And second, there were those instant cities represented by camps of soldiers during the Civil War. Hoy describes the scene in Washington, which was serving as a garrison at the beginning of the Civil War, as a hygienic disaster as young volunteers crowded in: "Having left mothers, sisters, and wives behind, they behaved as boys, whooping it up in the streets with the bugles and drums, getting drunk, firing weapons, relieving themselves in public and neglecting to wash. . . . Many of them had grown up on farms and had never been exposed to childhood diseases like measles; they promptly caught them."

These amateurs got sick en masse before even seeing battle.

This was nothing new. Disease had long felled more men in wartime than combat. What made all the difference during the Civil War was the fresh example of Florence Nightingale. Nightingale was the British nurse who proved during the Crimean War of the mid-1850s that deaths from disease in a military hospital could be dramatically reduced by basic sanitation. Inspired by Nightingale's experience, the United States set up a Sanitary Commission early in the progress of the Civil War to inspect and advise on the volunteer army. The secretary and chief executive officer of the Sanitary Commission was, oddly enough, Frederick Law Olmstead, the great landscape designer of Central Park fame.

The commission, like Central Park, was a huge success: The Union army suffered proportionally fewer deaths from disease than the Confederate army, whose government simply didn't have the resources for such a campaign; the public became acquainted with the concept of sanitation; and many volunteers returned home far more familiar with baths, clean clothes, soap, and the proper placement of a latrine than they'd been before the war. The Civil War proved it: Scrubbing oneself and one's surroundings could prevent disease, and an American health reform movement was off. Cleanliness was taught in the schools as well as in the army, and it became a vehicle for assimilating the many immigrants and rural migrants who soon made their way to American cities.

During the second half of the 19th century, science advanced to the point where it became clear that disease was not caused by dirt itself or miasmas produced by decaying organic substances, but instead by microscopic germs. An even higher standard of spotlessness was now demanded. And marketers of everything from tooth whiteners to clothes washers have exploited that standard ever since in order to get us to buy their products.

This argument really took off when designers figured out how to incorporate the look of spotlessness into the products themselves, making them streamlined and white. As Adrian Forty writes in *Objects of Desire,* a delightful series of essays about design, "In the decades since the 1930s, the aesthetic of cleanliness has become the norm in the domestic landscape . . . accepted unquestionably as the proper appearance for household goods of all kinds."

Ironically enough, this "aesthetic of cleanliness," which can be seen in fashions ranging from the all-white tiled bathroom of the early 20th century to today's stainless steel kitchen appliances, is spectacularly unforgiving, exaggerating the appearance of even a speck of dirt. But that is exactly the point, of course. The more aware we are of dirt, the more advertisers tell us dirt is shameful and disease-causing, the more money we'll spend to banish it.

To say that the messenger has a conflict of interest here is understating the case. But it's hard not to want to emulate the ageless and spotless people who inhabit the world of advertising, with their perfect white teeth and bouncy hair, moving through a house so perfectly polished, it's almost impossible to look straight on into its radiance without sunglasses.

It's also hard to imagine a place more antithetical to this gleaming notion of personal and household cleanliness than a vegetable garden. Sure, it's possible for a vegetable garden to wear the appearance of exaggerated order, but inevitably, most vegetables are planted over and over in soil that's enriched over and over and visited over and over by the gardener in order to harvest the fruits of his or her labor. In other words, more than any other kind of gardening, vegetable gardening involves intimate contact with the dirt.

Non-gardeners are like Victorian brides advised to lie back and think of England on their wedding nights: They assume that this contact is something that has to be endured for the sake of a greater good. On the contrary! Gardeners know that getting into the dirt is one of life's great pleasures. Good soil is absolutely magical. It is so full of life that scientists strain to make its biodiversity comprehensible, informing us that a single shovelful of garden soil holds more different species of organisms than there are aboveground in the entire Amazon rain forest. And the irony is that by avoiding the soil as if it were a source of sickness, we are making ourselves sick.

Immunologist Graham Rook of University College London is quite crisp in his assessment of the costs of dirt-avoidance: "If something is present throughout human evolution, it becomes something we need. Soil is certainly something our ancestors had a lot of contact with. We need it to be healthy. Without it, there's a gene/environment mismatch."

The evidence for such a gene/environment mismatch in modern life is crushing. In affluent, industrialized countries, the prevalence of diseases due to poor regulation of our immune systems—in other words, immune systems that gear up for a costly full-scale attack against harmless substances in the environment, our digestive tracts, or our own bodies—has soared over the last 30 or 40 years. These include allergic diseases such as asthma, rhinitis (or hay fever), and eczema; inflammatory bowel diseases such as ulcerative colitis and Crohn's disease; and autoimmune diseases such as multiple sclerosis and type 1 diabetes.

The prevalence of asthma in American children more than doubled in the 1980s and '90s, and 1 in 11 children now suffers from it. Asthma's prevalence is even more extreme in other Westernized countries, with 1 in 5 Irish 13- to 14-year-olds afflicted. The rates of allergic rhinitis are estimated to be about 40 percent in kids in the United States, Australia, Ireland, and the United Kingdom.

After observing that children who grow up in large families or who live on farms are much less likely to develop hay fever or allergic asthma, scientists developed something called the *hygiene hypothesis*. They postulated that our superclean lives in affluent countries leave us with too little exposure to germs that train our immune systems not to be paranoid and not to overreact to such harmless substances as pollen and cat dander.

Twenty years on, this hypothesis has been refined to the point where it's clear that the problem is not that we're too clean, but that we're not spending enough time in the dirt. It's not our exposure to germs in general that seems to matter. It's our exposure to particular organisms that are so common in mud, untreated water, and our own guts since the Stone Age that we evolved in tandem with them, organisms Dr. Rook has dubbed "old friends."

The "old friends" that have been identified as offering protection against allergies and autoimmune diseases are—like the Planet Earth in the sci-fi classic *The Hitchhiker's Guide to the Galaxy*— mostly harmless. They include benign soil-dwellers such as saprophytic mycobacteria, which break down the organic matter in the earth, as well as lactobacilli that are also out there in the garden breaking down plant matter and sitting in the cellar making sauerkraut and cheese. The "old friends" also include sometimes harmless organisms such as salmonella, hepatitis A virus, and parasitic worms such as hookworms.

Dr. Rook explains, "Our old friends have been around a very long time, since the Paleolithic. They were so common, they needed to be tolerated and so came to play essential roles in the regulation of our immune system. It's an example of evolved dependence."

In other words, if two organisms constantly in each other's company for eons both contain a gene that serves the same function, one may evolve in such a way that the redundant gene is dropped. Dr. Rook offers another garden-related example: "Humans are one of the few mammals not known to manufacture vitamin C. The genes that encode for the enzymes that make vitamin C were dropped because we were eating fruits and vegetables. Similarly, our evolved dependence on certain microorganisms turned on the regulatory aspect of our immune system."

Unfortunately, many of these old friends disappeared from our environment with the advent of indoor plumbing, pasteurized milk, chlorinated water, a concreted-over landscape, and a distaste for mud—in other words, the sanitary revolution. "In the mid-19th century in France," Dr. Rook points out, "people first noticed that aristocrats got allergic disorders rather than farmers. It soon became extremely fashionable to have allergic disorders. People would brag about their allergies because it showed their superior sensitivity."

If we can put our own sensitivity aside, peasant germs have been shown to have powerful effects on people suffering from the diseases of modern life. A trial of multiple sclerosis patients found that in those newly infected with parasitic worms, the disease barely progressed. Now the National Multiple Sclerosis Society is funding a trial of worm therapy.

"We've been interested here," says Dr. Rook about his own lab, "in mud bugs that drive regulatory pathways. In our clinical trials, a mud bug has been successful for dogs with eczema. Even *dogs* living in urban environments are now getting eczema!"

While the particular organisms that offer protection have not yet been identified, a number of studies have found that children who spend time early in life—or even in utero—in barns where livestock is housed or who drink farm milk (presumably unpasteurized) are powerfully protected against allergic diseases. A gardener like me, who views manure as miraculous in a vegetable garden, can only feel smug at such news.

Of course, the same cows and pigs that can keep us from getting allergic diseases can also expose us to potentially lethal bacteria. In my part of the world, runoff from a cow exhibit at the Washington County fair may explain how hundreds of people wound up being sickened by *E. coli* O157:H7 in the summer of 1999 and two of them killed by it, including a 3-year-old girl in heartrending fashion.

"There is no answer to that," says Dr. Rook. "So giving advice at the moment is dodgy. Yet, when there is a very large effect and you have almost half the population afflicted with immunoregulatory disorders, the damage in not encountering the protective organisms is conceivably greater than the small chance of encountering an *E. coli* that will make you sick."

Dr. Rook adds, "Nevertheless, I *would* be confident in saying mud bugs are good for you. So let the children play in the dirt! Let them grab a sandwich without washing their hands!"

Let's talk for a moment about why he is justified in that confidence, about why garden soil, unlike raw cow manure, is mostly harmless.

Why isn't dirt dirty? Because soil is by definition a waste treatment plant. All the lifeless stuff that falls to earth—dead plant matter, fall leaves, the wastes of animals and their bodies when they die—is decomposed by the creatures of the soil and, in the process, turned into the stuff of life, the nutrients that allow plants to grow.

The clean-up crew found in ordinary garden soil is so effective at eliminating pathogens that some of them produce our most important antibiotics. For example, bacteria called streptomycetes not only give soil its beautiful smell, they also produce streptomycin, tetracycline, and vancomycin, among other antibiotics, as well as medically important antifungal and antiparasitic treatments.

Penicillin is the product of another member of the clean-up crew, the fungi. Some fungi are single-celled yeasts. Others form rootlike threads called hyphae that group together into what are called mycelia, fungal networks in the soil, some of which produce mushrooms as their fruiting bodies. In his weird and wonderful book *Mycelium Running: How Mushrooms Can Help Save the World*, scientist Paul Stamets lists a number of ways that mushrooms can rescue us from the problems of modern life—including by trapping, killing, and eating a number of pathogens in our environment. He also writes about the first moment he observed mycelia through an electron microscope and suddenly had a new idea of their purpose: "I imagined that this fabric of fine cells could act as a biological filter." He has used such "mycofiltration" of water through beds of mushrooms on his farm in coastal Washington State to reduce the number of *E. coli* bacteria in runoff from his livestock, which threatened to contaminate his neighbor's shellfish beds below.

In the process of decomposing organic matter, soil microbes also generate serious heat that destroys pathogens. The temperature inside a compost pile can reach 165°F—not hot enough to cook a turkey properly, but hot enough to reheat leftovers. One year, I had a giant pile of ground-up maple leaves and lawn clippings delivered for me to spread on my garden. Even in the frosty November air, the pile was steaming dramatically. My kids and I all pushed up our jacket sleeves to stick a bare arm into the hot center—and nobody wanted to hold that arm there.

Good garden soils also bind and break down pollutants and keep them from being absorbed by plants, which is good news if, like most of us, you are not gardening in recently cleared virgin forest, but in a spot that's been used by humans over the years for sundry purposes. A Canadian teenager won a science prize in 2008 by identifying soil bacteria that could rapidly decompose plastic bags. Fungi, which decompose the toughest organic matter such as the lignins in dead wood, are also great moppers-up of pollutants. Paul Stamets calls them the "grand molecular disassemblers of nature," able to break down complex toxins into simple, benign substances. He tells me, "This includes toxins deposited on the soil by air pollution, such as the residues of coal-burning power plants." Fungi can also degrade pesticides, preservatives, diesel oil, even chemical warfare agents. While I wouldn't necessarily *site* my garden on a spot where there had recently been chemical warfare, it's good to know that if I did so inadvertently, somebody's on the job.

As I said earlier, I feel instinctively that my soil is clean and never worry about picking a gritty arugula leaf in the garden and eating it right there, grit and all—or letting my kids do the same. What does deserve caution, however, are animal wastes and remains that haven't been composted or otherwise worked on by soil organisms. While it's not a common story for people to be sickened by a home garden, *Lancet* reported in 1992 that a Maine woman and three children were infected by *E. coli* O157:H7 after the woman had used manure—presumably fresh—in her garden all summer from her own cow and calf.

Some people worry so much about such a possibility that they refuse to use manure at all in their gardens. To me, the manure cycle is the cycle of life. We care for the grazing animals we've domesticated, and in return, they enrich the soil that produces the plants that feed us. Besides, the combination of straw and manure is magic in my experience. This is what you get when you muck out a stall, and it also happens to be the perfect recipe for compost, a lovely balance of carbon-rich dried grass and nitrogen-rich wastes.

Since *E. coli* seems to thrive in the guts of cows fed the unnatural diet of grain rather than grass, you might want to stay away from manure produced by a big commercial meat or dairy operation. (You also might want to stay away from it because vegetable crops can absorb the antibiotics in the manure of animals routinely fed such drugs.)

But the key thing in avoiding lethal *E. coli* in manure seems to be allowing enough time for the cleaning process to work. Scientific studies have varied in the length of time they've found *E. coli* persisting in soil and manure, everything from mere days to a scary 21 months. However, organic soils—with their thriving clean-up crews—seem to get rid of the germ faster, as does either heating things up by composting or letting the manure sit in the lower temperatures provided by, say, winter.

Ultimately, the USDA's National Organic Program regulations for organic farmers seem pretty sensible even for home gardeners: "Raw animal manure must either be composted . . . or incorporated into the soil at least 90 days before harvesting an edible product that does not come into contact with the soil or soil particles and at least 120 days before harvesting an edible product that does come into contact with the soil or soil particles."

In recent years, a retired neighbor of mine who raises alpacas has tractored loads of relatively fresh alpaca bedding down the road for my garden (the best possible kind of neighbor!). I'd let the stuff sit in a pile all summer and then fork a sheet of it over the whole garden in November and let it sit through the winter. Since my first crops were not even planted until 5 months later, I didn't worry about it. I'd have had even less to worry about if I'd have dug the bedding into my garden soil, rather than just let it sit on top.

However, there are no guarantees with manure that you will never run into a stray pathogen. Some gardeners forgo manure entirely and go vegan by feeding their soil kitchen scraps, straw, hay, fall leaves, wood chips, or nitrogen-rich cover crops. That works, too. The important thing is making sure your soil has plenty of organic matter.

In my almost 2 decades as a gardener, I have had two big revelations about my soil that have led me to a much simpler and more sustainable way of doing things: one, that the best soil amendments come from a field or barn, not a factory; and two, that it's better to mulch the garden every year than to dig it.

The first life-changing event occurred after I'd been gardening for 4 or 5 years. One spring, my neighbor, who kept three sheep for decorative purposes, offered to let me have some of their bedding for my garden. I took "some" to mean about 40 wheelbarrow loads of straw and sheep manure, wheeled very quickly across the road before she could protest. I just forked it into my soil lightly and instantly found myself in the middle of a Jack-and-the-Beanstalk transformation, where the seeds hardly fell out of my hand before I was being whipped about by vegetables reaching for the sky.

That was the first time I'd ever seen explosive growth in my vegetable garden.

Until then, I'd been buying stuff for my soil at the hardware store, peat moss and plastic-bagged manure so thoroughly broken down, it would have been more honest to label it humus, which is the persistent stuff that's left *after* the soil microbes finish their job. Humus and peat moss are great in that they improve the soil's structure and its ability to hold water—though peat moss, which is harvested from bogs, is a natural resource that renews itself excru-ciatingly slowly and probably shouldn't be used in the garden. But neither one offers much in terms of nutrients, so I'd also been adding bagged fertilizer to feed my plants. It cost a fortune and though it was organic, it looked and smelled like nothing I'd ever seen in nature, a stinky light brown powder.

If you simply compared labels, the bagged fertilizer offered a far greater concentration of nutrients than the sheep bedding, so you'd think that the explosive growth would have fallen to the purchased products. Ask soil microbiologist Dr. Elaine Ingham why it didn't, and her first guess is, "There was no life in any of it. It was inert. Or there might have been the wrong kind of life. The stuff sealed in plastic might have gone anaerobic and begun favoring organisms that could cause all kinds of diseases."

She adds, "With the fresh material, you were probably adding fungi and bacteria and good-guy nematodes that would bring your soil back to life." Some soil creatures are shredders and decomposers born to shred and decompose, not to process powders. For the first time since I'd made the garden initially, I was giving them something to work on. They were in turn feeding my plants, and growth of my vegetables was an expression of the joy underground.

It would take volumes even to attempt to describe the web of life in the soil, so let me briefly sketch out one small portion of the activity underground—the nitrogen cycle—to help you understand how beautifully a living soil works. Nitrogen is an essential ingredient of proteins and DNA. It is one of the building blocks of life, and, as I mentioned earlier, it's often the limiting factor for plant growth. Even though nitrogen is all around us, abundant in the air and in the bodies of living creatures, it's present only in forms that plants can't use. Without soil bacteria that "fix" the nitrogen of the air and other creatures that "mineralize" organic nitrogen so that plants can take it up, we wouldn't be sophisticated machines programmed by DNA. We'd be big piles of nothing.

The nitrogen-fixing bacteria include those called rhizobia that set up shop in nodules on the roots of legumes such as peas, beans, and clover and provide nitrogen in exchange for sugars produced by photosynthesis. This symbiotic relationship is the reason legumes are often used as "green manures." When they are grown as a cover crop, they add nitrogen to the garden.

Mycorrhizal fungi also set up shop among the roots of most plants and trade nutrients, including nitrogen, for the carbohydrates produced by photosynthesis. Because their thin rootlike hyphae extend far beyond the plant's roots and are able to penetrate smaller spaces than plant roots, they can bring nutrients from distant places within reach.

And though nitrogen is stored inaccessibly inside the bodies of bacteria and fungi in the form of complex proteins, it can be unlocked by predators such as protozoa and nematodes that eat the bacteria and fungi and then secrete wastes that contain nitrogen in a plant-usable form. Other bacteria return nitrogen as a gas to the atmosphere, keeping the cycle going.

We humans learned to bypass this cycle 100 years ago by converting atmospheric nitrogen into fertilizer ourselves. What microbes do casually, we can only do with tremendous heat—930°F—and tremendous pressure, and tremendous environmental costs, including the overproduction of the greenhouse gas nitrous oxide and the leaching of this nitrogen into waterways, where it promotes blooms of algae that remove oxygen from the water, killing off marine life and causing enormous dead zones, such as one in the Gulf of Mexico. If overused, especially in combination with insecticides and herbicides, artificial fertilizers, which are salts, kill some soil creatures and reduce the diversity of life in the soil.

Dr. Glover of The Land Institute compares adding artificial fertilizers that bypass the pathways through the life in the soil to "hot-wiring a car." He adds, "We try to do at a large, industrial scale what is typically supplied in healthy soil at a small scale. Soil creatures are evolutionarily much better equipped to carry out those processes. But the conventional mind-set is still so dominant that fertilizer companies want to get soil to be as inert and sterile a medium as possible, to eliminate the complexities of the soil."

The arrogance of that program is just stunning. No one who writes about the soil can resist quoting Leonardo da Vinci on its mystery—"We know more about the movement of celestial bodies than about the soil underfoot"—and apparently, I can't either. Only a tiny fraction of soil species have been cataloged so far. It's been estimated that only 5 percent of the species of fungi have been described and only 3 percent of the species of nematodes. The digestive tracts of soil animals are constantly yielding new species of protozoa, and there may be a million distinct bacteria species in a single gram of soil.

We know so little about the relationships between these creatures that even scientists can't figure out what to feed them when they hold them in captivity. In his delightful introduction to the soil, *Tales from the Underground: A Natural History of Subterranean Life*, Cornell University soil ecologist David W. Wolfe points out that "Even in modern laboratories, scientists are lucky if they can come up with a mix to culture and study *1 percent* of microbes found in a typical soil sample. This poor success rate is due in part to the complex interdependence between subterranean organisms. They can't survive when isolated from their neighbors."

I take it as a matter of faith that every single one of these unnamed creatures has some subtle but essential purpose in the web of life—and that there are unforeseen consequences to eliminating any of them from the picture.

Says Dr. Ingham, "The soil food web is a system developed by Mother Nature over the last billion years. She's had time to get it right. Who are we to think we've learned everything we need to know in the last 60 years?"

Instead, Dr. Ingham recommends that any gardener hoping to build beautiful soil and grow what she calls "Alaska-sized vegetables" start by being both humble and attentive. The first requirement is understanding who's in control in a healthy garden—and it's not the gardener. It's the crops.

Plants, the subtlest of all chemical factories, can exude a large variety of chemicals from their roots. The science of these exudates is just being discovered, but it suggests, says soil ecologist Dr. Wolfe, that "plants are orchestrating things underground."

Dr. Ingham explains, "They use these exudates to wake up exactly the right microbes, that in turn release exactly the micro-nutrients they need. And they get those nutrients at the right moment, unlike the nutrients in water-soluble chemical fertilizers that are present in a big burst and then quickly leached away."

Plants can also use these exudates in different ways to fend off threats, including by attracting benign bacteria and fungi around their roots that protect them from pathogens and other thugs.

Dr. Ingham crisply sums up the role of gardeners in helping plants get what they need: "Our *only* job as gardeners is to maximize the diversity of organisms in the soil."

Dr. Glover compares healthy soil, vividly, to the wildlife-rich plains of the Serengeti: "You want to have lions and cheetahs as well as gazelles. If it's all gazelles, you have overgrazing and problems with disease, as there is no control over the weaker ones."

The best ways for the gardener to encourage a rich soil ecosystem are to plant a range of crops and add organic matter to the soil that will harbor and feed that biodiversity.

Dr. Ingham recommends using your eyes and nose to judge the value of soil amendments, pointing out that ideally compost looks like a "70 percent cocoa bar of chocolate." Darker than that, the compost may well have been overcooked into lifelessness. "You should see some white strands of fungal hyphae. It should have a good, rich mushroom smell."

Though Dr. Ingham consults with farmers and wine-makers around the world on their soil biology and offers precise assessments of the balance of organisms in their soil, her recommendation for home gardeners unwilling to pull out a microscope is blessedly low-tech: "Monitor your plants. See if you're getting the growth you want. If not, add some nice, lively compost. Make sure when you dig up a shovelful of soil, you see passageways for air. There should be earthworms in it, and not just 1 per shovelful, but 5 or 10."

This leads me to my second great soil revelation: Mulch, don't dig. It occurred about 5 years ago. I had moved a few years earlier to the city of Saratoga Springs and made my vegetable garden at the charming dump of a weekend house we'd bought on 15 acres in the country. After the sod was plowed up, I added a truckload of farmyard cow manure to the garden, a big pile of which my friend Loren had hanging around. He warned me it was "weedy." I saw only its lovely 70 percent cocoa color and deemed it fertile.

"I've never had a problem with weeds in my garden," I said airily.

It did not take long for the cow manure to demonstrate the arrogance of that statement. Keeping up with the weeds is one thing when the garden is behind your house and you can yank out the creeping Charlie, dock, and plantain every evening. It is another thing entirely when you are not around from Monday to Friday. I tried to do what I usually did, which was allow the vegetable seedlings to grow to a respectable size by early July and then put down a loose mulch of straw over the bare ground.

But I couldn't weed fast enough even to get the straw down on weed-free earth, and even when I did, more weeds germinated anyway, just shrugging off the light sweater of straw I'd placed over them. I had never truly understood the phrase that I'd hear from country people, "The garden got away from me," until then. The garden got away from me. By the end of the summer, I was hunting for food in a forest of weeds.

The next year, I swore I'd keep up. I turned my soil over by hand as I usually did, exposing even more weed seeds to light, which germinated explosively once again. Needless to say, the garden got away from me again. In a state of despair, I consulted Ernie Niles, whose crew has mowed my country lawn for the last 2 decades.

Ernie is a big, slow-talking guy on a noisy lawn tractor whose relationship with me for at least a decade consisted of not much more than the occasional wave above the din. But time has taught me that Ernie is a font of country wisdom.

"You need more mulch," he said.

"Do I need more straw? Should I make it deeper?"

He shook his head. "Grass products are a problem. They always generate some weeds of their own. I'd suggest wood chips or fall leaves."

I was as shocked as if he'd recommended bourbon or scotch for my kids' sippy cups. The gardening lore is that neither leaves nor wood chips belongs in a vegetable garden. What I'd read about wood chips is that since they are nitrogen-poor, the microbes decomposing them have to steal nitrogen out of the soil in order to work, so wood chips rob your soil of fertility. What I'd read about leaves is that they are too acidic for a vegetable garden.

These are exactly the kind of myths to exasperate horticulturalist Dr. Linda Chalker-Scott of Washington State University—the myths that turned her into another of the very few scientists communicating with gardeners in her nonsense-busting *Informed Gardener* books. She points out that with wood chips, the nitrogen deficiency occurs only at the interface of the soil and the mulch, which makes them superior in discouraging weed growth. Similarly, she tells me, "If you put down a leaf mulch, there might be an acidic interface between the leaf mulch and the soil. But a few inches even of oak leaves is not going to acidify a huge amount of soil."

Ultimately, I trusted Ernie more than my books, and when he offered me a giant pile of fall clean-up matter from one of the big properties he mowed, I took it. It was mostly ground-up maple leaves, with a bit of mown grass mixed in. I first spread my lovely alpaca bedding and then I forked truckloads of leaves over my garden.

The next spring, to plant my seeds, I just took the handle end of my shovel and ran it down a line in the bed, pushing the mulch aside and creating a row. That summer, my garden was entirely different. The leaves were amazing at blocking light to the soil, so weeds didn't germinate. The ones that did germinate grew only weakly and were easy to pull. Sometime in July, I stopped dead in my tracks. What *was* that on my soil?

It looked like streusel on a cake: worm castings, a layer of them literally everywhere. I had clearly made umpteen earthworms extremely happy, and I knew that this was a powerful sign that I was doing the right thing.

In fact, earthworms are not just a sign of soil health. They *make* healthy soil. They are the best possible ally to anybody hoping to grow a little food. In her charming book *The Earth Moved: On the Remarkable Achievements of Earthworms*, my friend Amy Stewart suggests that earthworms are practically unpaid farmhands: "They work alongside humans, extracting a life from the land."

The earthworms that I'd engaged were pulling the organic matter I'd put on top of the soil into their burrows and eating it, mixing up the soil as they went, aerating it and enabling it to hold water. They were also concentrating the nutrients that passed through their bodies and putting them within reach of plant roots. They were even excreting calcium carbonate, the same ingredient in agricultural lime that raises the pH of the soil, turning acidic soils more neutral.

"Add lime" was one of the first pieces of advice I got as a gardener, since I garden in the acidic forest soil of the Northeast, and vegetables are supposed to prefer somewhat less acidic soil, where the availability of nutrients is maximized. But I haven't given the pH of my soil a thought in years and have noticed no languishing whatsoever on the part of my vegetables. I'm assuming that the earthworms are taking care of it.

From the moment that I saw my soil covered with worm castings, I decided to stop digging over my garden every year and let the earthworms do the job for me from now on. I instinctively understood that they are much subtler gardeners than I will ever be. Even the sloppy hand digging I'd been doing would undo their work, as well as the work of moles and beetles and fungi with their mycelia. To rototill, God forbid, would just completely smash it all into smithereens.

I still find plenty of work for my shovel—I like using my shovel—in planting things, getting rid of the weeds that do appear, and fighting the grass at the edges of my garden.

Dr. Ingham suggests tilling only where and when there is a good reason to do it—to prepare a smooth bed for delicate seeds or to remove weeds—and then as gently as possible. "This recreational tillage of the whole garden area," she says with gentle scorn, "makes no sense."

You won't find any tilling in the garden of Dr. Glover, either, who has been dubbed by *Nature* magazine one of "five crop researchers who could change the world" for his work to turn wheat into a perennial crop that will require far less energy, fertilizer, and plowing than the annual wheat planted today, making large-scale agriculture far less damaging to the environment in general and the soil in particular. In his own garden, too, Dr. Glover explains, "I don't like turning the soil. I don't like the idea of disturbing all those nice channels."

Paul Stamets, too, the great champion of the fungi, says, "Sheet mulch."

Mulch mimics nature's own method of soil enrichment, which is from the top as the leaves fall and the grasses die back in winter and the animals leave their wastes and finally bodies behind. Nature knows what she is doing. Mulch does everything for me. It serves as fertilizer and weed-eliminator. It keeps the soil moist and cuts way down on the amount of watering I have to do, allowing me to use a sprinkler on a timer twice a week without worrying about things drying out in between, even in the hottest week.

A mulch also makes my huge garden a reasonable proposition with a few hours a week of work. First of all, I don't have to dig over 1,872 square feet every spring. And I don't have to spend every Saturday and Sunday thereafter weeding, unhappily, like a gardening Sisyphus who no sooner cleans up the joint than a million tiny new weeds appear. I get to use the time I save on housekeeping on more creative activities such as planting and cooking.

With a mulch controlling water evaporation and weed growth, my garden can also look after itself for a summer week or two with no attention from me. This allows me to behave like an adult instead of an obsessed child and to win the respect of my family by separating from my crops for a bit, so we can all have a high time visiting our friends Gail and Dan and their children, who have a romantic place on a lake in the Adirondacks, or our friends Martha and Tom and their children, who have an equally romantic place on the coast of Maine. I love my garden, but I also love my friends and their waterfront houses.

A mulch makes my garden beautiful, too, giving it a polished, restful look that a garden of bare soil never has, since such a garden is almost never without an unsightly stubble of emerging weed seedlings. My garden never looks unkempt—or never so unkempt that 10 minutes of plucking the few weeds that do appear won't turn it into a beauty queen.

I like mixing up the materials I use as mulch within a year and from year to year. Before my conversation with Dr. Ingham, I'd imagined that by doing so, I was allowing no nutrient to build to excess. Now, I see that I may well be encouraging the biodiversity of my soil by asking it to break down different raw materials.

One year, I will just use Ernie's leaves. In another, I'll use just my neighbor Herb's alpaca bedding, though last year, I faced some competition with my friends for that, applied it too thinly, and my garden was weedy again. In a lucky year, I might use both. I'm thinking of trying wood chips this fall, a weighty form of mulch that ought to make it difficult for any weed to rear its ugly head.

Despite Ernie Niles's anti-grass feeling, thickly applied straw or second-cut hay that doesn't contain a lot of seeds would also work. Ruth Stout, the tart old character who became a late-life gardening guru in the 1950s with a "no-work" perpetual mulch method, used spoiled hay for her mulch, applied it 8 inches deep, gardened in the nude, and claimed that her method allowed her plenty of time for cocktails and naps.

If I had a lot of manure or compost—relatively broken-down stuff—I'd put that next to the soil and then cover it with something coarser that is more likely to keep down the weeds.

Organic farmers sometimes employ cover crops as a living mulch, using them to fill in bare spots in the garden, or mowing them down before planting time and allowing their remains to cover the surface of the soil. I have never tried this because in my short-season climate, not enough of the garden is vacant long enough for me to grow a cover crop.

It's possible, too, to go even more natural on the mulch front, as Japanese rice farmer and organic movement guru Masanobu Fukuoka did. Fukuoka pioneered a beautifully orchestrated no-till, "no-work," polyculture method of farming when he returned to his father's farm in 1938 after a brief career as a plant pathologist. He recommended growing vegetables on otherwise unused land in a "semi-wild" way, simply cutting a swath in the weed cover and then scattering the vegetable seeds, placing the cut weeds as a mulch over them. The weeds were then cut down two or three more times during the season as they grew back—but never grubbed out—until the vegetables could hold their own among them.

Radical. Too radical for me. I know that weeds have their own purpose, in that they reach for different minerals in different places than the cultivated crops and enrich the soil after they die or die down. But in my own garden, I've seen vegetables that fail to grow properly in competition with weeds. And I must admit, I like my garden to be pretty. So no living mulches for me—but don't let me stop you if you want to try them.

Whatever you do, just don't leave your soil naked. At this point of life, I actually cringe now when I see unmulched soil. It's like seeing a child outside in the wintertime without a coat. Indeed, without some kind of covering, either of living plants or dead organic matter, the bare earth erodes, loses its carbon to the air, contributes to greenhouse gas emissions, dries out, and becomes infertile.

The truth is that the greatest crisis of natural resource depletion the world faces at the moment may not be peak oil at all. It may well be the destruction of good soil. Today, soil is being ruined all over the globe by compaction from the monstrous equipment used in industrial farming; by sterilization caused by chemical pesticides and herbicides; by erosion caused by over-tilling and the careless removal of natural vegetation; and by the influence of our carbon emissions, which are bringing drought to some of the poorest places on earth. Without good soil, there are only deserts and starvation. History shows that one of the surest ways to end a civilization is to wreck its soil.

Yet even severely degraded soils can be brought back to life with a bit of mulch. In the hot and arid Sahel, south of the Sahara in Africa, farmers are making the dead land live again using the simplest techniques, like putting composted manure into pits. The manure draws termites, which begin tunneling the soil so it can hold water and air and support life. The pits collect scarce rainwater and allow grain crops to grow, as well as trees that can then provide shade, wind protection, and a leaf-fall mulch.

If a mulch can remake that land, it can remake yours.

So at the risk of seeming like just another bossy garden writer,

I am going to have to insist that you feed the earth, cover it with organic matter, take care not to rough it up too much as you work, and respect the species known and unknown underground.

I also recommend that you feel a little saintly while you are at it, too. In your own backyard, you will be doing your small part to save your own species. Because we will all go very hungry indeed if we don't stop looking at soil as something distasteful and start seeing that it is the key to life.

six

Beauty

Prettier Than Sod and Shrubs Any Day

When I was 11 years old, I went to Germany to spend the summer with my Aunt Rose. I learned a lot of things that summer: how to play a fantastic card game called *Schafkopf,* how to say the word "squirrel-tail" in such an obnoxious Bavarian accent that it would crack my uncle up, how to spot the bolete mushrooms that my aunt would turn into a delicious soup at 100 yards in a drizzly forest at dawn. But the most important thing I learned was that there was no inevitability to the New Jersey landscape I was growing up in, that we humans have choices in shaping the world around us.

Rose was only a year older than my mother, and they'd been rivals since birth, good-looking women who'd played tug-of-war over clothes, boyfriends, their daddy's love, the whole business of life. They were both ambitious and hardworking, but in opposite directions. As I mentioned earlier, my mother is a member of a self-selecting group, those people who aren't born Americans but decide to become them. She was a true capitalist, an independent operator, a career girl through and through, even after she had children and left New York City and moved to New Jersey. She worked in accounting at the Western Union headquarters 2 miles away from our house for years, loved her job, and was ferociously good at it; it was her efforts as much as my father's that allowed us to live in a big new house.

My Aunt Rose, on the other hand, applied the same furious energy and precision to housewifery and spent her whole life a few miles from where she was born. From morning until night when I was a kid, Rose was running around her ancient house breathlessly, scrubbing her floors, stirring her pots, ironing her sheets. And her duties included a very large garden that unfurled down and away from the back of the house like the most beautiful Persian carpet ever made.

Rose lived in a village organized on the medieval European plan, with the houses and stalls huddled together on a hillside near the church and the fields fanning out from there. Though it was in the middle of town, just a few steps up from the church, her garden felt very private. It was walled in by the neighbors' cow-stalls on two sides, and to this day, a whiff of fresh cow manure brings back the pleasantest of memories to me. Her yard was terraced down a slope, with tool sheds and a small lawn on the first level, a chicken coop and vegetable rows running parallel to the slope on the next level, then a step down and more vegetables and a hedge of currants at the end.

As an 11-year-old, I had all kinds of powers in that garden. I could run to the bottom of the yard on impulse and eat the sour little currants by the back fence. I could pick a cucumber when I wanted a cucumber and chew it whole without asking permission. I could reach sleepily out of my bed in the morning and pull wonderful tiny purple perfumy grapes off an ancient vine growing up the house and eat them in bed. And if I felt lazy on a Sunday afternoon, I could sprawl in the grass while my handsome and funny Uncle Fritz roasted one of Rose's delicious chickens, stuffed with parsley from the garden, on a spit.

This place was heaven to a kid. It had never occurred to me before then that a yard could be so beautiful, yet beauty was not the goal at all. It was all about saving a penny and not being wasteful or lazy. It was the ultimate purposeful yard. And it was lovely.

Of course, you could argue that my mother's yard was beautiful, too. Like most of the yards in my New Jersey town, hers had a big, well-groomed lawn interrupted by evergreens in curved beds, with some thin new-growth woods at the edges. The ingredients were typical: lots of spiky, unfriendly creeping blue junipers, lots of arborvitae, and a bunch of rhododendrons that would bloom briefly in prom-dress colors in spring, giving the yard its only flowers, and then sulk for the rest of the year. But in my mother's yard, everything was particularly healthy and meticulously maintained. Every evening, the second that dinner was finished, my mother was out of the house like a flash, watering, weeding, fertilizing, and mowing until night fell. She wasn't doing the same things in her yard as I do in mine, but clearly, she got the same sense of peace out of it.

For everybody else, however, the yard was meaningless. You couldn't swim in it. Given the steep grade of the property, you couldn't even really play in it. You couldn't find enough flowers to fill a vase in it. Since there was no fence or hedge, you couldn't make out with your boyfriend in it—not away from prying eyes, anyway. And you certainly couldn't eat out of it.

In fact, there was no excitement *anywhere* in the landscape I grew up in, no flowers, no food, no color, no privacy, no art, no chickens pecking for worms, and no running on the perfect grass allowed. And that makes it a totally typical American neighborhood.

We are overwhelmingly a nation of landowners: Sixty-two percent of America's housing units are single-family detached houses, and by definition, they are all surrounded by some sort of yard. Yet most of us demonstrate zero imagination about the ways a piece of ground might be enjoyed. Our yards are generally landscaped once, never to be thought of again, and never to be softened up by any ongoing experimentation and discovery on the part of the homeowner.

Whatever interest there is often takes the form of an excessive concern for control and neatness, to the exclusion of bugs, bees, or kids playing tag, sometimes announced by little yellow flags wearing skulls and crossbones warning that pesticide has been applied. Clover, a nitrogen-fixing plant that enriches the soil, is herbicided into oblivion for the sake of the lawn's consistency. In the development where my mother lives today, island beds were installed specifically to *keep* kids from playing on an open lawn. It's easy to read in most yards something approaching paranoia about the natural world, as well as the desire for impeccability raised to lethal standards. There is no fruitfulness or mystery or joy, no sense of welcome to the other species that might possibly share such a yard, the way the birds share my vegetable garden.

Nature is a cornucopia, but the average American landowner is a miser who disapproves of the feast.

What I didn't understand as a dissatisfied child was that the yard I was growing up in was merely an expression—you might even say the culmination—of very deliberate ideas that had shaped the American suburb from its inception in the mid-19th century and that continue to dictate the prevailing fashions in yard-dom today. The lack of geometry, the failure to fence or hedge, the superneat haphazardness—these were all part of the suburban plan from the beginning. As Lewis Mumford explains in his brilliant and prescient 1961 book *The City in History,* the first suburbs embodied Romantic-era ideas of "studied accident and willful wantonness"—in other words, nature unbridled by human necessity.

The look of the American suburbs had its origin in the gardenless parks of the English Landscape School. Thanks to the influence of tastemakers like William Kent and Capability Brown, 18th-century British aristocrats suddenly found their formal geometric gardens fusty and embarrassing, and ripped them out in favor of free-form lawns and vistas and the occasional Greekish outbuilding. British garden writer and designer Penelope Hobhouse describes this carefully careless style rather wittily: "Its grassy meadows, serpentine lakes, gently contoured hills, and artfully arranged clumps of trees seem the very model of Englishness, almost indistinguishable from the 'real' countryside."

Three hundred years later, with their forest evergreens and their sod, many of the suburbs of North America are almost indistinguishable from "real" woods and meadows except, of course, for the houses and the asphalt. Interestingly enough, this suburban style is so much the prevailing style in America that even in my small city of Saratoga Springs, where the yards are often not much bigger than the yards in brownstone Brooklyn, it's all about the grass and the arborvitae: the Great North Woods writ super-small.

"This is not a garden," these yards say. "This is raw nature, only neatened up. The homeowner does not labor in this space." The purposelessness of these yards is the very point of them. The suburbs are not the country, where people make their living off of the land. They are not the big city, to which the adults commute in order to make money. They are a place whose only object is the good life.

In his classic history of the American suburbs, *Crabgrass Frontier*, Kenneth T. Jackson hits upon the meaning of the meaningless yard: "Although visually open to the street, the lawn was a barrier—a kind of verdant moat separating the household from the threats and temptations of the city."

In other words, a desire to separate oneself from the world lies at the very heart of our suburban nation. It explains everything about the way our big yards look, and why we have so little interest in them. And that desire to separate oneself is completely dependent on the car, of course, because a car is the only possible way to navigate a landscape of widely spaced homes with any kind of efficiency.

It's all so 20th century. And it's *over.*

Nothing on earth is more obsolete than the idea that it's possible to retreat from the world's problems in a suburban hideaway. We're coming up against practical limits imposed by greenhouse gas emissions and a finite supply of fossil fuels, fresh water, and land. Climate change, the global financial crisis that began in 2008, and fear of a deadly flu pandemic are making it clear even to the well-insulated rich that we citizens of earth are more or less in this together.

All revolutions involve aesthetic readjustments, as yesterday's arbiter of fashion—the Lehman Brothers banker in his Hummer, Marie Antoinette in her shepherdess costume—becomes today's source of outrage. And if we are in the midst of a sustainability revolution, then it's time for a new eyeglass prescription when it comes to our squandered yards. Wasting millions of acres of fertile soil nationwide is not pretty. Treating nature as if it's just another annoyance to be kept at bay like a shouting kid or barking dog is not pretty. What's pretty is showing some interest in the earth, even interacting with it.

The recent "outdoor room" fashion in landscape design may represent the first dawning recognition that yards are not just negative space and they ought to serve a function besides just soaking up weed-and-feed. Before it was shut down by its parent company in 2009, even the elegant garden purveyor Smith & Hawken was peddling outdoor televisions, which are, on the one hand, the ultimate in nature-blind stupidity—entertainment for people who simply don't know how to *be* outdoors—and on the other hand, perfectly comprehensible. Why not use the yard for something you enjoy?

I find all kinds of yards beautiful, as long as they are used. Yards that create a strange mood are beautiful: I remember one ridiculous but magical yard from my childhood that was all jewel-colored gazing globes, painted gnomes, and topiary yews. Most towns have a crazy plant-loving old person or two. In the neighborhood where my husband grew up in Silicon Valley, it was a Portuguese lady who turned her yard into a jungle, so densely planted and overgrown the house could hardly be seen. Crazy old lady yards are often beautiful in an unhinged way, and I'm sure that in a few decades, I will have one myself. Yards for play are sometimes beautiful: I'm partial to a nice sparkling swimming pool myself and scheme constantly, though unsuccessfully, about finding the cash for one. But the most beautiful yards in my opinion are productive, whether that productivity takes the form of food or flowers. I'm talking about yards that accept and celebrate the gifts of nature rather than senselessly spurning them.

While I like flower gardens, vegetable gardens represent the more powerful makeover opportunity for the unloved American yard. Not only are they ultimate in usefulness and the richest possible way to connect our land and our lives, they also add precisely those aesthetic qualities that our domestic landscape is most desperately lacking.

First of all, even the smallest vegetable garden usually has a certain classical geometry going for it, since the most practical way to manage vegetable crops is by planting them in rows and narrow blocks separated by straight paths. The truth is, you have to be a genius to create an attractive free-form landscape, something without obvious rules that nonetheless has its own logic, which is why most suburban yards, with their island beds and curving paths, generally fail the beauty test. But it doesn't take any kind of special eye to make a pleasing landscape if you use a bit of geometry. So believe it or not, rather than lowering the tone of the average American yard, vegetable gardens have the potential to raise it by adding some badly needed formality to the disorganized scene.

Vegetable gardens also provide something else sadly missing from many yards, which seem to consist mainly of trees and grass, and that is a middle ground: elements at shoulder or head height, such as staked tomatoes or trellised pole beans. The plants themselves are so various and gorgeous in terms of their shapes and leaf-forms and colors that they are an instant antidote to the sterility of the American yard. They also tend, by midsummer, to riot a little, making the vegetable garden an aesthetically interesting place where a controlled shape dukes it out with uncontrolled growth.

Vegetables offer one more quality that the American yard is generally lacking: the beauty of anticipation. We love our inert evergreens that always look the same, but if I had to live in a yard that was nothing but lawn and evergreens, I think the dire lack of drama there might spur me to pursue more self-destructive forms of drama in other parts of life. In most yards, once the obligatory flowering shrub or two finishes its thing in spring, nothing happens until the leaves drop, except that the grass grows and is mowed and grows and is mowed. Vegetable gardens, on the other hand, are constantly altering. They will give even the most frequent pass-ersby something new to gawk at every day.

Even the most humble, traditional vegetable garden is beautiful—and by that, I mean a small patch of ground ripped out from the sod and planted with a few straight rows of toma-toes and lettuces. And on the other end of the scale entirely, there are potagers, hyper-aesthetic and highly formal gardens in which the vegetables are mainly planted for looks, not for food. Vegetables can provide the materials for a really grand garden, such as the one Joachim Carvallo made at Chateau de Villandry, in the Loire Valley, in the early years of the 20th century. The vegetable garden is basically an enormous quilt with clipped boxwoods marking its squares, which are then filled in every year with umpteen plants of a single vegetable. The effect is monumental.

So the whole idea that vegetable gardens ought to be hidden away out back with the shameful stuff like pool pumps and garbage cans is absurd. If the only place I had to garden was in a front yard, I would make the garden in the front yard. But I would certainly fence a front-yard vegetable garden to discourage passing dogs from marking my cabbages, and I would be very careful to make it substantial-looking and handsome.

How can a beginning gardener make a beautiful vegetable garden, one worthy of the front lawn, even if relegated to the back? Let me tell you about the first time I was ever thunder-struck by the beauty of a vegetable garden, because that garden offers some important lessons. It was the first time I ever visited Bob Nunnelly and Gerald Coble's house in the rural hamlet of Battenville, New York. They were friends of friends, and kindly invited my husband and me over when we first rented a house in the country and were thinking about leaving New York City for beautiful Washington County.

We arrived after dark at their house, an 18th-century tavern with enormous rooms, high ceilings, unpolished floorboards, rough plaster, and lots of amazing art everywhere, much of it made by the two of them. While I was supposed to be chatting, I was actually surveying the place with intense curiosity. There was an awful lot to take in, because Bob and Gerald have the subtlest, warmest, earthiest, and yet most elegant possible taste in furniture, décor, art, and movies, as well as people. At some point in my surreptitious tour of their enormous kitchen, I saw a wonderful black-and-white photograph hanging on a wall.

It was a picture of a large vegetable garden taken down its strictly measured and slightly raised rows—a dramatic perspective that drew the viewer in, made more dramatic by the fact that the garden was covered in mist, and the photograph seemed to be inviting you into a state of enchantment. Behind the garden was an ancient barn, unpainted, with a sagging slate roof. Before the barn, there were the vaguely human shapes of well-pruned fruit trees lifting their few limbs above their shoulders. A few small, exquisite little evergreens popped out of the planting beds. Otherwise, they were empty.

It was the most beautiful place I'd ever seen, timeless and mysterious. And I couldn't imagine where the people lived who were sophisticated enough to make such a garden. Italy? France? The moons of Jupiter?

"Oh, my God!" I exclaimed. "Where *is* this?"

Bob laughed. "Out back."

It was their vegetable garden. The photo was by an old friend of Gerald's and Bob's, Boston-based photographer Ben Watkins, whose pictures of landscapes and architecture are often so inspired. Here's the important point about that photograph: It was taken in the off-season. The garden was outrageously beautiful, even without vegetables. And this, in my humble opinion, is what every vegetable garden should strive for.

Most vegetables are annual crops. They start out as a tiny seed or seedling and then proceed to swell rapidly over the summer, until by harvest season, they are really impressive. My garden is at its most magnificent right before a frost hits, usually in late September. That means, however, that vegetables look like nothing in the winter, and next to nothing in the spring. So vegetable gardens need substance.

If you're lucky, you might have a backdrop like Bob and Gerald have—a beautiful 18th-century house and ancient barns—to lend weight to the scene. But most of us aren't that lucky, and Bob's and Gerald's garden would be glorious even if it sat beside a trailer.

That's because they have also included all kinds of interesting permanent features in their planting beds, inspired by Italian gardens and by the harsh winter climate of upstate New York, which otherwise would obliterate the garden for 5 months at a time. There are not just the fruit trees I mentioned, but beach ball–sized boxwoods and giant, looming arborvitae standing in for Italian cypresses at the perimeters.

Gerald also grows many things in pots, including beautiful old citrus trees that he moves out of the house in spring. These pots, too, add shape to the garden when it's nothing but a bunch of hair-sized seedlings. Some of the mystery and magic of their garden is about scale: The biggest pot of rosemary you've ever seen in your life lines a path, and an oxymoronic giant dwarf Alberta spruce anchors one end. Gerald also builds all kinds of rustic trellises out of sticks and twine to support peas and beans. Again, they give the garden shape and verticality in the spring when the plants are not offering much of either.

But it's not all about structure. Their garden is also beautiful for its blooms. It is casually edged by ornamentals such as oriental poppies and tulips and many dozens of rugosa roses that add color to the crucifers. The vegetable garden is also visually connected to the more purely ornamental areas of the yard, with its paths leading to vistas outside and its borders lending their shape to other features, including a spectacular allée of arborvitae guarded by two giant cement dogs. The whole garden feels both coherent and expansive.

Ultimately, Bob's and Gerald's vegetable garden is beautiful because it makes a really beautiful statement about life: that there is no reason that the most mundane of tasks—feeding yourself—can't be done with some elegance. In fact, their garden makes you wonder whether the most elegant thing in the world might not be a really nicely grown crop of beans.

Ask a professional—Marin County, California, landscape designer Michelle Derviss—what makes a vegetable garden beautiful, and she lights on exactly the same qualities that Bob and Gerald have emphasized. "Good architectural bones are essential even in Northern California," she tells me, "where there is no dormant period in the garden, because the garden is also never hidden by snow."

Her own front-yard vegetable garden has a circle-in-a-square shape, with a big pot marking the circle's center, which is then surrounded by a ring of gravel, surrounded in turn by vegetables, which are bounded by a low, square, carefully clipped hedge of boxwood. The boxwoods anchor this potager into a highly gardened yard, and in a really fun, personal note, white ceramic hands that Derviss sculpted reach out of them. "Sometimes they hold my Felco pruners," she says. "At Christmas, they hold Christmas balls."

She also advises making sure that the vegetable garden fits into what she calls "the narrative—the house and garden should be speaking the same aesthetic language." And she adds, "You might as well plant flowers you can pick as well as vegetables." She makes room for lobelias, calendulas, and sweet peas amidst the vegetables.

My own garden doesn't begin to approach these two gardens in terms of its sophistication. But it's lovely, too, in a delightfully ordinary way. It's got some architecture in a cedar picket fence at the perimeter and a little garden house full of muddy shovels that I've stained a dark bluish violet. I have simple cast-iron arches over the main paths for my pole beans, which I think are wonderful, especially in late summer when they are covered with heart-shaped bean leaves. I like structures of any kind that raise the vegetable garden out of two dimensions into three. When I was younger and broker, I used to go into the woods and saw off saplings in spring and tie together 10-foot sections of them to make teepees for my pole beans. These structures were beautiful, too, and they had the advantage of being free.

Also anchoring my garden are four small fruit trees along one of the main axes—'North Star' pie cherries, which top out at 8 feet and so never will cast a lot of shade—and currant and gooseberry bushes lining another. The currants, in particular, are a beautiful plant, with leaves shaped like a child's hand.

I'm also a big fan of flowers in the vegetable garden for the glamour factor. Again, you have to find the right companions for vegetables—flowers that won't mind the rich soil and steady moisture that vegetables need. Roses certainly fit the bill. The cast-iron arch at the main gate of my garden sports a pair of 'William Baffin' climbing roses. They have semi-double flowers in an unsubtle yellow-pink, with an open face that reveals their sunny yellow heart.

Tall dahlias are also happy companions to vegetables. They're not hardy where I live, so I plant the tubers in spring and then lift them after a frost and store them in Rubbermaid tubs filled with wood shavings in my basement in the winter. Dahlias have hollow stems that will fold over if they are not supported, so the tall ones all need to be tied to a fence or stakes. In return, they bloom on and on for me, with flowers in an amazing range of sizes and shapes and colors, from July until they are cut down by a frost. I often plant a large maroon and white dahlia that looks fantastic in bouquets with purple basil. Lately, I've been planting a scarlet ball dahlia with such a careful honeycombed shape, it looks too regular to be real.

Annuals like zinnias and sunflowers also look great in a vegetable garden. You might want to steal an idea from painter Claude Monet's garden at Giverny and use lots of trailing nasturtiums to crawl into your paths. Nasturtiums require nothing more than pressing seed into the soil after the last frost. Their leaves and flowers are edible, too, which amuses my kids. Nasturtiums grow well in poor, dry soil, and these are theoretically the conditions they prefer, but I've never had a problem getting them to grow and flower in the beautiful loam of my garden.

I also love self-seeders that pop up and surprise me every year like Johnny Jump Ups, the occasional wild mullein, nicotiana, and a fantastic double pink opium poppy. Opium poppies need to be thinned and given elbow room or they will grow in a stunted fashion. But if you thin them, they will produce a beautiful blue-green plant 3 feet tall, with big succulent buds that bend their heads gracefully towards the ground until they are ready to open, huge colorful flowers, and a seed pod that is one of nature's finer pieces of engineering, designed like a sugar caster with a row of holes on top to shake out ripe seed as the wind blows.

And then there are the vegetables and fruits themselves, chard with brightly colored ribs, red cabbages with an icy-blue blush, chartreuse or burgundy lettuces, chives with their purple pompom flowers, crimson-flowered fava beans, grape vines with their lush pentagon-shaped leaves, peach trees with their wonderful long, languid foliage and peach-colored blossoms—these are all so beautiful that they can earn a spot in a garden planted for looks alone. That giant-leafed, primitive dinosaur-breakfast called rhubarb is so stunning that some members of the family are planted purely as ornamental perennials. Pole beans, particularly varieties with colored flowers such as 'Scarlet Runner', are beautiful plants that will easily grow 8 to 10 feet tall over the summer, with large heart-shaped leaves, sprays of flowers, and delicious pods hanging down like prisms off a chandelier. They are wonderful on a structure over a path. If I had no space for a dedicated vegetable garden, I'd make room for these things in my flower beds.

Of course, the requirements of a tiny vegetable seedling and a 15-year-old shrub or a well-established flowering perennial are not the same. Most vegetables need more regular watering and richer soil to perform well and room enough to soak up the sun and grow like crazy over the course of the summer—which is why vegetables are usually given their own space. But if the only space you have is in an ornamental bed, by all means, scratch some lettuce seed into the front of the border and see what happens.

I have to admit, I find the cheery reds of the tomatoes, the glossy blacks and lavenders of the eggplants, the sophisticated burgundies of the radicchio heads as striking in late summer as even the most dramatic flowers. Vegetables are beautiful. And the explosion of color they represent is telling us something significant. The chemicals the plants produce that give rise to these startling colors have important health effects for us. Many of them are antioxidants, which are thought to protect against both heart disease and cancer.

In *On Food and Cooking,* Harold McGee offers a helpful rule of thumb: "There is a useful guideline for estimating the relative healthfulness of vegetables and fruits: the deeper its color, the more healthful the food is likely to be." Jere Gettle, the young entrepreneur who founded the Baker Creek Heirloom Seeds company, points out that heirloom varieties often have unusual colors. His catalog is full of photographs of fruits and vegetables styled as artfully as *Vanity Fair* styles starlets, the incredible chartreuse of a 'Boule D'Or' melon, for example, vibrating against the gray-brown of unpolished floorboards. "We get different health benefits from different colors," he says. "The more colors, the better for you!"

So there is nothing irrelevant about this kind of beauty. There is nothing irrelevant whatsoever about the beauty of a vegetable garden, even though a pretty one may well announce that its owner is a pleasure-loving fool. We may well owe our ability even to *perceive* beauty to edible plants.

Our primate ancestors are among the few mammals with trichromatic vision—the ability to see reds, as well as blues and greens. Scientists theorize that this ability evolved because it enabled monkeys to pick out ripe fruit and the youngest and tenderest red-tinged leaves against a background of mature green leaves. Without vegetables, there might not be any ancient Greek pottery, or Rita Hayworth in flaming Technicolor, or Velasquez princesses with challenging expressions on their faces and coral-colored bows in their hair.

Vegetable gardens are all lovely, in my opinion, lovely by definition—as long as somebody's weeding them. But the loveliest vegetable gardens I see are the ones that include something beyond mere utility that the gardener has chosen and clearly finds meaningful, such as a thick stand of sunflowers, or an interesting fence, or a piece of metal sculpture done by a friend with a blowtorch, or a planter made out of a truck tire filled with pansies, or a birdhouse. It really doesn't matter what.

What matters is the refusal to separate the beautiful from the useful. This is the exact opposite of the statement most American yards make today, which is that if it's useful, it's not beautiful. But in the backyard at least, both utility and beauty require human imagination, a willingness to engage with the world, a love of life.

It's not merely the wonders of nature that are celebrated in such a garden. The best of humanity is readily apparent there, as well.

SEVEN

The Kids

What They'll Take Out of the Garden

Ask my children what my vegetable garden means to them, and you'll instantly get a snappy answer even from the 7-year-old: "It means you're always too busy to spend any time with us!"

Well, that shows *me*.

And I'd end this chapter right here, if I thought my kids' experience of the garden was all about resentment. But if it were, I suspect that my offspring would not be so damned insistent, every year, on getting their own section of my garden to plant.

Every Memorial Day weekend, each one of the three claims a yard-wide row 16 feet long. If I allowed them more, they'd take more, but even motherly love has its limits.

And let's not be sentimental here. There is nothing idyllic whatsoever about the ensuing scene. Generally, there is considerable bickering in the nursery over how many flats of seedlings each one can pick out. They want 100 apiece, whereas I actually have some idea of what will fit in the space allotted. There are also fights about how many truly ugly annuals they are allowed to stick into my pretty garden. I always cave and then spend the season wincing at the orange marigolds. This is then followed by much diligent planting on their part and a lot of shouting on mine, as they drag the hose over my tiny, fragile seedlings and leave the water running where it washes away my arduously mulched path.

None of this is easy for me. I'm not fastidious about much, but I am fastidious about my vegetable garden. If I didn't think letting my kids inside the garden fence was important, nobody under 30 would ever be allowed there. But I do think it's important. I think it's so important to let kids into the garden that I've added a third garden to the two gardens I already do, my city ornamental garden and my country vegetable garden: a school garden at Lake Avenue Elementary around the corner from me in Saratoga Springs. Of course, this last one is shared, very enjoyably, with another mother and 18 insanely excited schoolchildren.

To me, gardening with kids is all about opening their eyes and their taste buds to food. My children wander into my vegetable garden throughout the summer, feeling a sense of proprietorship because I've allowed them room for their marigolds and their cucumber obsessions, and graze the place. By 2 years old, they were able to recognize basil and rosemary. And they'd pull off a leaf here and there and sample them. They'd go out and pinch off a stalk of arugula and chew it right there. As for the currants, gooseberries, and strawberries—they'd simply eat the place clean.

It's not just my kids, either. Studies of school garden programs have shown that kids who garden eat more vegetables—though not necessarily that their preference for vegetables changes radically. But somehow the vegetables make their way into their mouths.

The way my kids behave in the garden has been a great relief to me, since I happen to have that motherly conviction that vegetables are essential to everybody's health, except maybe to the Inuit, who traditionally get most of their vitamins and minerals second-hand, from raw whale and seal.

My older children, Milo and Georgia, twins aged 12, have always eaten vegetables as a matter of course, probably because I was icily manipulative with them when they were babies. I'd simply feed them the vegetables first, while they were really hungry, before we'd move on to meat and starch. If they didn't eat their vegetables, there was no dessert. Early in my parenting career, completely exhausted by my twin toddlers, I'd gotten an excellent piece of management advice from the CEO I worked for, David D'Alessandro of John Hancock. "You have to be like the mob with kids, Michele," he'd said. "Strictly business. Once you get angry or anxious, it's all over. They've won." David is a very wise man, and since then, bribes and threats have been an important part of my mothering style. You didn't eat your spinach? Sorry, no ice cream. It's nothing personal, just business.

Then I had my youngest child, Grace, a Carole Lombard–ish miniscule funny blonde, whose steely character within a petite pretty package means that she simply cannot be manipulated under any circumstances. Grace, now 7, is immune to bribery and laughs off all threats. And she happens to prefer boxed macaroni and cheese and boxed cereal to the entire cornucopia of nature. My own homemade baked macaroni and cheese? She's having none of it. And if you don't give her the creamy bland or sweet carbohydrates that she likes, she'd rather starve, thanks. Grace is perfectly willing to skip dinner and then eat three bowls of breakfast cereal ravenously the next morning, and do it again day after day. Even as a Thumbelina-like 4- or 5-year-old, she'd go to other people's houses, where the children got boxed macaroni and cheese as a rule, and eat so much for such a tiny person that the parents would express astonishment when I came to pick her up.

In other words, even as a theoretically powerless small child, Grace found it easy to evade my program in the kitchen. So thank God for the garden! She's at least spent her early childhood grazing for greens there.

That's the first advantage of a garden for a parent concerned about his or her kids' diets. You probably will get some vegetables into your kids, if only through their absent-mindedness as they wander around and thoughtlessly stuff a certain amount of the place in their mouths.

The second advantage is that your kids are likely to eat a wider variety of vegetables if you grow them. Studies of younger kids confirm that if they garden at school, they are more willing to try different vegetables. After all, once they learn that homegrown peas are a little like candy dots and that tarragon tastes like a licorice stick, they are more likely to give the next strange thing they pull out of the soil a chance.

J. Harrison of The Food Project, which offers teenagers from wildly different backgrounds summer jobs in sustainable farming in Massachusetts, is always amused by the transformation that occurs over the course of a summer as kids acquire new tastes on a farm. "Teenagers love to try new things on a dare," he tells me. "The bad side is that you'll occasionally see a young man trying to pretend he's not in obvious pain. I'll have to say, 'You ate a jalapeño *again*?'"

My kids might complain bitterly every night about the experimental nature of my cooking, where I'm always pushing into new frontiers involving collards and parsnips and spices, when they'd rather have a plain steak and mashed potatoes. But if you get them out of the house and into a restaurant they suspect might be good, as happened to us recently several times on a trip to Quebec, they *will* order the venison pâté, the tempura-fried smelt, the pureed turnips, the celeriac salad, and the duck. Even Grace. Maybe especially Grace.

My garden has clearly turned my kids into more panoramic eaters than they might be. This is important to me because I see it as predictive of their future enjoyment of life. I want my children to be the kind of people who say yes to the unfamiliar. I think it's civilized to be a bit of an adventurer, though admittedly, I'm not much of a skier or mountaineer, and my own adventures mostly take place on my plate.

However, at the risk of contradicting myself, I have to say that it seems equally important for my children's future health and happiness that while they are sampling the entire range of the edible, they also become discriminating about the *quality* of what they choose to eat.

I would be horrified if my kids were intellectual snobs or material snobs—not bloody likely, given the leaking plumbing and rotting porches of their undercapitalized home—but I want them to be food snobs. That's just self-preservatory, as self-preservatory in the age of unending shelves of Doritos chips and pudding cups as a similar snobbery probably was to our Cro-Magnon ancestors, when fussiness about the taste of a berry or a mushroom might have kept them from poisoning themselves.

Making me into a food snob was one of the biggest favors my European mother did for me. She refused to eat processed foods because they tasted appalling to her, and because I didn't eat processed foods at home, I never got used to the taste of the factory and that new-car smell of industrial solvents and lubricants and plastics you get from factory foods. Admittedly, I might have had an easier time of it as a kid if the Ragú and Chef Boyardee I was served at my friends' houses didn't make me gag. But I am extremely grateful that I learned the difference between delicious and dishonest early.

I've had ample proof that I am having a similar influence on my kids. My husband once took my older children on a long hike in the Adirondacks. They'd bought sandwiches at a roadside store on the way there. By the time they'd reached the mountaintop after hours of marching and climbing, they were all ravenous. But my daughter Georgia took a bite, opened the sandwich, saw that it was processed turkey, not the real thing, and quietly threw the sandwich off the mountain.

Georgia, my horse-loving girl who at age 12 happily wears dirty rags off her bedroom floor and never bathes unless ordered to, is fussy only about food. She won't eat the apples from the supermarket and she won't eat the green beans. She knows what fresh from the garden smells and tastes like and won't settle for much else. She claims that even her pony Trusty can tell the difference between the carrots I've grown and supermarket carrots and likes mine better. And in this culture of abundance—such overabundance that you can't go anywhere in America without seeing lots of kids who are handicapped by their own body weight—knowing enough to say "No, that's *not* good enough to eat" might be the single most important thing any child could learn about food.

Some of my friends argue that worrying about the quality of the food your kids eat is a borderline decadent preoccupation of the educated and lucky. But I don't see it that way, probably because it was my mother who taught me how to eat, and as I mentioned earlier, she passed a very hungry childhood in wartime on a filthy pig farm. My mother's example suggested that until we face absolute starvation, we humans are surely justified in having a bit of pride about what we're willing to put in our mouths.

A discriminating palate is not a luxury, the way that bluefin tuna or filet mignon is a luxury. While it is expensive to feed a big family out of the Whole Foods store or a farmers' market, it is not expensive to garden for one. You can satisfy a tableful of discriminating palates all summer long with a few dollars' worth of seeds.

It's no accident that some very poor places in the world have very rich food cultures, since they are cultures that brook no waste, and people garden on every scrap of available land at every conceivable moment during the year. My husband, who has spent some time in China, raves about the unbelievable range and quality of the food he was served there, by people so poor, they were burning dung to heat their huts. The poorest city I've visited in Europe by far—Naples, Italy—has some of the most magnificent food I've ever eaten. Stumble into a workingman's trattoria in

Naples, and for 4 euros, you will be served a plate of pasta so good, the sun-infused glow of the local olive oil and tomatoes will take days to wear off.

And in a poor neighborhood in America's poorest big city, Detroit, I met an amazingly ambitious vegetable gardener in her eighties, Lillie Neal, whose grandmother considered learning how to discriminate between good food and not-so-good an important part of her education, and never mind that this was in black rural Mississippi during the Great Depression. "My grandmother," Lillie told me, chuckling at the irony, "knew all *about* organic food. She showed me that greens raised with fertilizer don't taste right, while greens raised with cow manure are good."

Plant a garden, and kids instantly learn what flavor *really* is. My daughter Georgia's 12-year-old friend Kate Dennett, a wiry little spitfire with a shockingly deep voice, will relate in dramatic form every disaster that has befallen her family's suburban back-yard garden, including chipmunks that dine brazenly on strawberries in full view of their windows. But ask her what the point of the garden is, and she'll bellow, "The strawberries taste SOOO good."

However, the very idea that it's important to turn kids into little food critics—particularly poor kids—enrages some people. Caitlin Flanagan, *The Atlantic*'s resident gadfly on all domestic subjects, kicked up a storm in 2010 in both the worlds of food and education by attacking a movement in California to incorporate gardens and cooking into the public school curriculum. To Flanagan, teaching underprivileged kids about beautiful food when they could be learning reading, writing, and arithmetic is the ultimate liberal folly, an example of a silly "let them eat tarte Tatin approach to the world."

Let them eat tarte Tatin? That ought to be a rallying cry. It's certainly my rallying cry.

Let's let *all* the kids eat tarte Tatin, city kids, country kids, suburban kids, rich kids, poor kids, the kids of fundamentalists, the kids of hedge fund managers. Let them all taste the difference between a pastry made at home with good butter and apples from the yard, and a Pop-Tart, so they can decide for themselves.

Here is what's so important about good food: It is satisfying in reasonable quantities. And junk foods, well, they offer the hint of something longed for, but never the full experience, seducing one to eat more and more and more, in hopes of arriving at a destination that never appears—that mirage called flavor.

We need to teach our kids to be critical eaters, because it is the only way they can protect themselves from a food culture that is provably insane. One out of three American children between ages 6 and 19 is overweight, according to the National Health and Nutrition Examination Survey, and nearly one in five is fully obese. And because of it, increasing numbers of kids are subject to the health problems that used to belong only to decadent middle age, such as type 2 diabetes, high blood pressure, high cholesterol, and fatty livers.

American kids are eating so badly, in fact, that those eating habits threaten to reverse one of the great triumphs of human ingenuity, the near-doubling of life spans during the 20th century. In an essay in the *New England Journal of Medicine,* pediatric endocrinologist Dr. David Ludwig summed up the problem with devastating simplicity: "Pediatric obesity may shorten life expectancy in the United States by 2 to 5 years by midcentury—an effect equal to that of all cancers combined."

Despite the appalling evidence that we are not, as a nation, doing the right thing by our children, we still feed our kids as if they are too stupid to tell the difference between fresh food and not, and as if what they consume doesn't matter. I know really good cooks who eat beautiful food themselves, but then give the kids frozen pizza pockets and soda for dinner as if the game is not yet being scored. Their children only rarely eat anything green. Ask these parents about it, and they shrug helplessly, as if they have no influence on what their kids are willing to eat.

Admittedly, it is difficult to defeat an entire culture from the trenches of your own kitchen, maybe impossible. More to the point, it is exhausting trying to persuade kids to eat well when the stores are full of processed foods beckoning to them from the aisles, when their friends eat nothing but processed foods, when their schools serve such appalling food in the cafeteria, when the most well-meaning teachers reward their students with candy.

But we parents are not helpless. While we cannot force-feed our children food they refuse to eat—at least not under the criminal code as I understand it—we do have this much control: We are in charge of what's offered. And what's offered generally has some influence on what gets eaten.

So a vegetable garden is the best way I can imagine to take charge. Not only does the food that comes from the yard taste better than anything that can be bought, the garden has the curiosity factor on its side. It has worms, toads, flowers, things that grow in surprising and dramatic ways, such as Brussels sprouts and rhubarb and corn. It's simply an interesting place—and kids respond to that. And the ritual of pulling something out of the soil lends a certain cachet to what's on the plate. Grace, who would never eat asparagus, was suddenly amused last summer by the way that asparagus grows, with pencil points pushing themselves up out of the ground, and she had fun snapping off the stalks for her dinner, because they do snap audibly and announce a job well done. After that, I was forced to set aside most of the asparagus I cooked for her.

Of course, I like having my kids in the garden not just because it's a place to find good food and to learn how to eat, but also because it's a place to experience the seasons and watch the bugs. Kids need to spend time in nature, not only for their physical health, but for their mental health, as a place they can be away from electronic devices and noisy peers and either think quietly or avoid thinking entirely.

And let's face it, it is very difficult to be happy without sunshine and birdsong and perfumed air and the sound of the wind moving through the leaves, and those things are available in abundance in a vegetable garden or orchard. At least, I would find it impossible to be happy without them, and my heart breaks for kids whose days are spent moving between school and the inside of their house and back again.

Dr. Candice Shoemaker of Kansas State University told me the story of a boy who inspired her to go back to school to study the health effects of gardens on people. She was a recent college graduate in floriculture who hoped to have a greenhouse business someday selling flowers and potted plants. But the only job she could find was taking care of a small farm and orchard attached to a home for about a dozen severely disabled kids. "One little boy named Danny arrived," she explains. "He had severe cerebral palsy. His grandmother had taken excellent care of him from the time he was a baby, but she had just died. He was grieving terribly. He would just get off the school bus and sit in his wheelchair.

"But when spring came, he wanted to garden with me. I'd help him get out of his wheelchair and he'd lie in the grass and weed and harvest with his hands flying. After he'd been there 3 or 4 months, he was really transformed, not a withdrawn sad kid, but a happy, fun little boy. It was so rewarding for me, and it made me see that it could be pretty powerful to grow food." The greenhouse idea was set aside, and Dr. Shoemaker was soon back in school, studying horticultural therapy to figure out the mysterious connection between health, happiness, and a garden.

My kids, too, have had some ecstatic experiences in my garden, particularly when they were little. When my twins Milo and Georgia were small, it was a battle for me even to be allowed to garden, the two of them in concert were so demanding. I could hardly pick up a shovel before they were running off in different dangerous directions, or asking for a drink or the bathroom. But the May when they were 3, we had a breakthrough. There were shrieks of delight when they figured out that every time I stuck my shovel into the soil, I revealed worms. I'd have to pause and let them pick the worms out of the clump of soil before I was allowed to move on, until their fists were full of poor wriggling worms trying to escape all this attention, and they were running after me into the rows, shouting, "More worms, Mommy, more!" So they let me dig, in a manner of speaking. But I still wasn't gardening very effectively—I was laughing too hard.

Of course, there are many ways for kids to experience nature, and I wouldn't argue that my vegetable garden is at all superior to the things my children do on their own, like take off all their clothes and cool off in the shallow stream on our country place or catch frogs in our pond. Certainly, the most satisfying hours of my childhood were not spent helping my mother weed her landscaping, but were spent away from adults with my toes in a brook, catching salamanders and tossing bread crumbs to crayfish. Journalist Richard Louv had a bestseller a few years ago with his book *Last Child in the Woods*, which describes a condition of the American childhood he calls "nature-deficit disorder," namely, the fact that too many kids get too little opportunity for unstructured play outdoors.

And the garden is not unstructured, just the opposite in fact—it's a place where your mother is always telling you where to step and where not to. But it is a good place nonetheless to feel out what it means to be human in the natural world that we rely on for our sustenance. It's a good place to figure out that we are not so different from the other creatures who also look to the garden as a source of food, starting with the insects and the toads, spiders, and birds who find those insects tasty. Learning to take care of a row of marigolds and cucumbers is not bad practice for being an adult human in a tiny, crowded world that we are currently treating much too roughly.

Plus, there is also the science to be gained. While I am by no means out there in my garden behaving as any sort of teacher—I'm more of a hysterical scold, and *get offa the planting beds, wouldja?*—there is no way any child can spend time in a garden without learning loads about genetics, botany, entomology, and climate science, and depending on the sophistication of the gardener and the kid, microbiology and atmospheric chemistry.

So the idea that gardens have no place in schools, particularly schools that serve mostly underprivileged kids, amazes me. Before anybody dismisses a school garden, they ought to interview Principal G. Asenath Andrews of the Catherine Ferguson Academy in Detroit, who is responsible for educating not just underprivileged kids, but underprivileged kids who have had one of life's tougher breaks—and that is to find yourself a single mother while you are still a child yourself. The Catherine Ferguson Academy is a very unusual public school in that it is devoted to teenaged mothers and their babies, and it happens to have an unusually funny, earthy, and imaginative principal in Andrews, who instantly bristles at Caitlin Flanagan's idea that school gardens are a distraction for poor kids who need to concentrate on the basics: "Why is it that people only talk about a back-to-basics education for poor kids? It's a class issue. Poor kids are the ones who are prescribed rote memorization, never rich kids. Well, of *course* you can't do a garden *instead* of reading, writing, and arithmetic. But certainly you can do it *in addition* to those things, as a jumping-off point for a lot of new ideas."

Principal Andrews is in no sense undemanding of her students. College acceptance is a requirement for graduation from Catherine Ferguson. And the garden at Catherine Ferguson is fittingly ambitious, so ambitious that it's a blooming farm. There are horses grazing on what was once a running track. Endless beds of vegetables ring the oval perimeter. There's a full-fledged orchard. There are rabbits; there are chickens; and there are goats for milking. A few of the teachers grow almost all of the feed for the farm on a vacant lot across town and get the students to help bale the hay.

Ask her what the farm does for her girls, who are learning carpentry skills there and raising barns as well as carrots and babies and Andrews says, "By rights, we should be off the charts on every science exam, since our students *get* it at a fundamental level. But we're not," she sighs. "Just as a practical matter, the girls only come to the school when they become pregnant, some of them not until the 11th grade."

Of course, Andrews is not just responsible for the mothers, but also for the babies and toddlers they bring to school, and it is completely obvious to her that the garden is extraordinarily good for them. "First of all, it's so fundamental, having good food out there. You can get little kids to eat anything they grow. And show a 2- to 3-year-old the bugs in the soil with a dollar-store microscope, you'll hear, '*Huuuh!*'—that long intake of breath that is the sound effect of amazement, a sign of a new thinking process. It's a sound effect that I hear sometimes from the girls, and never once in a staff meeting." She chuckles. "If I ever hear it in a staff meeting, I'll know I can retire."

Andrews points to research that suggests that by age 3, poor kids have heard 30 million fewer words than kids in middle-class families. She once told me that that 30-million-word deficit keeps her up at night.

"We're trying to teach teenagers to *talk* to their babies. Poor babies don't hear enough complex language," she says. "Well, there's a whole vocabulary attached to a garden that these teenagers can share: compost, worm castings, microorganisms, mulch."

I suspect that Andrews and I look at a garden in the same way: as an endless frontier with endlessly beautiful specifics. I've certainly noticed that the elementary school kids I've been gardening with are constantly adding to their own word hoards by asking endless questions: "What's kohlrabi? What's compaction? What's nitrogen?"

What they all are, is bits and pieces of a really interesting world.

In my experience, the science of growing engages kids, and so does the commerce, really, really. Just put a copy of a beautifully photographed catalog like Baker Creek Heirloom Seeds in front of a kid, tell him he can pick out a couple of packages to order, and watch him have the shopping experience of his life.

Two summers ago, for the first time, my children set up a farm stand with the food and flowers they'd grown and made a few twenties a week at it. The farm stand unleashed a torrent of creativity and speculation—and even more adamancy the next spring that a certain portion of the garden was theirs.

Ah well, I like having them out there. I think my kids like being out there with me, too, even when they are not contemplating selling something on our front stoop. As long as they stay off my seedlings, an unrushed air of peace generally reigns in the garden, the way it does nowhere else in our ambitious lives.

I suspect that my children get a lot out of the garden, as much as they may complain about their mother's obsession with it. But I think that on balance, I get even more out of gardening with kids.

The kids in the Lake Avenue Elementary School Garden Club certainly taught me a lesson last September when it came time to harvest the fruits of our first year. At that point, I was mainly focused on what had gone wrong. Unlike my own garden, this garden is not a dictatorship, and I'd have made different choices than the group made in terms of the site selection, the fence purchased, the soil preparation, and the feasibility of gardening in sandy soil without easy access to water.

However, as the person who lives closest to the garden, I did most of the maintenance over the summer break. I spent a lot of time lugging watering cans down the street, muttering imprecations. I was also unhappy that the vegetables weren't growing as well as they should have. Despite my decree that we needed 3 yards of compost for the little garden, my colleagues had only bought 1 yard, and the soil clearly wasn't rich enough. Plus, 2009 was a record-awful growing season in my part of the world, with rainstorm following rainstorm.

There was also the fact that I only really took care of the garden until mid-July, when I was suddenly too buried in work even to raise my head and have a look at it. The cucurbits got mildew when sopping wet weather was followed by 2 dry weeks in which I didn't water. I also never managed to do some other things I'd intended to do: weed, edge, rip out the gone-to-seed salad and broccoli and replace them with fall crops.

When I surveyed that garden in early fall, I could only see failure.

But on a Wednesday September morning, our first scheduled garden meeting of the new school year, six or seven of the shorter members of the Garden Club showed up and saw the mature garden for the first time.

I swear, I heard Asenath Andrews' *"Huuuh!"* sound from every one of them. They filled bags full of cherry tomatoes, arugula, basil, beans, lemon cucumbers, zucchinis, carrots, and radishes, shouting in amazement as they picked and pulled. These kids weren't grousing about how the pole beans seemed a little sparse or the greens were woody. They were thrilled to be harvesting the fruits of their labors.

Their excitement at the transformation of their seeds and seedlings into something they could eat was really moving. It seemed like a miracle to them.

It is a miracle.

EIGHT

The Never-Ending Education

Why You'll Soon Be as Much of an Expert as Any Expert

The wisest thing anyone ever said to me about the vegetable garden came from CR Lawn, the 64-year-old founder of my favorite seed company, Fedco Seeds: "In the long run," CR offered, "your work is rewarded if you pay attention to details. In the short run, you never know."

This nugget of wisdom arose as CR and I were both complaining about the rainy summer of 2008 in the Northeast. With his long white beard, CR looks something like cartoonist R. Crumb's Mr. Natural character. But unlike Mr. Natural, CR wears his guru status very lightly. He's witty, soft-spoken, humble, wry. And he's right. You do never know: 2008 was soon followed by the even colder and rainier summer of 2009.

CR's welcome letter in the 2010 Fedco Seeds catalog said it all about 2009, a dismal year on all fronts including the economic: "I think of our thousands of new customers," he wrote, "who, in the face of the Great Recession and the revealed inadequacies of our food system, decided for the first time in many years, or ever, to plant a garden. Only to be rewarded, at least in New England, with the worst growing season in 40 years. . . ."

Ha!

How bad was 2009? It was so bad, that for the first time in my gardening career, most of my heat-loving crops, including melons, cucumbers, and peppers, failed to do much of anything. It was so bad, thanks to a nasty disease called late blight that thrives in cold, wet weather and targets members of the nightshade family, including tomatoes and potatoes, that every single one of my 18 tomato plants had to be yanked and the leaves on my second crop of potatoes shriveled as soon as they poked their heads aboveground. A summer without fresh tomatoes, a winter without stored potatoes . . . it was not misery on the scale of the Irish potato famine, which was also caused by late blight, but 2009 was nonetheless a season full of sorrows.

And I was far from alone in such sadness. Farmers all over the Northeast were yanking out their tomatoes and lamenting the economic loss.

Vegetable gardening is easy, in the sense that for relatively little time and labor and expertise, you can grow a lot of beautiful food. But it is the furthest thing from foolproof. You will fail with certain crops in certain years. It happens to professional farmers and it will happen to you.

That's because no matter how methodical, rational, and alert you become personally as a gardener, you are forever subject to the whims of your far less stable partner in this endeavor, Mother Nature.

In fact, climate scientists tell us she is becoming moodier than ever, thanks to our greenhouse gas emissions, which are likely to provoke more severe weather of all kinds and to alter our growing seasons and what have long been considered sensible planting dates. While some gardeners are going to have to find a way to water their gardens in the future despite persistent drought, others of us are going to have to figure out how to grow Mediterranean crops despite increased precipitation.

We're all experts in the garden, right up until the moment that we're not. Screenwriter William Goldman once famously wrote about Hollywood, "Nobody knows anything." In other words, not even the most careful student of the movies—or most anxious studio executive—can predict what is going to succeed in the future.

Nobody knows anything in gardening, either. That's not to say that there aren't people who have enormous stores of knowledge about vegetable growing. I like to think I have a certain amount myself. But the predictive value of that knowledge—and therefore its usefulness—is limited, without precognition about what the weather will be like and a familiarity with the particular spot to be gardened.

Every single time you try a new crop or new variety or new plot, you risk failure. Even with the tried and true, a year of strange weather can make decades of experience meaningless. Longtime gardeners understand that a certain amount of disappointment comes with the territory, but beginners don't know this. And the one thing that is most likely to keep beginners from becoming gardeners is taking this disappointment personally.

It's the common thread in every conversation I've ever had with somebody who tried a garden once, but felt it was unsuccessful. For example, I recently ran into a neighbor in the supermarket, someone who'd moved out of New York City to Saratoga Springs with her family in just the last few years. She isn't an experienced gardener, but she happens to be an experienced pickler. "I love making pickles, but I got hardly any cucumbers last season," she said, looking abashed. "I'm sure I did something wrong."

"Nobody had nice cucumbers last year," I grumbled. "It wasn't warm enough for cucumbers."

"You're just saying that to make me feel better," she said.

"No, really, I'm *not*," I insisted, shivering in the chill of the dairy aisle, which reminded me unpleasantly of the summer before. "It was a bad year for cucumbers."

When I talked to CR early in 2010, as Fedco's seed orders were just picking up steam, he noticed that many of his new customers from the previous spring—there were loads of these, because Fedco's sales increased 50 percent from 2007 to 2009—were not coming back. Like my neighbor, these first-timers clearly didn't understand that they hadn't done anything dreadfully wrong. They'd just picked a dreadful year in which to start.

They blamed themselves, and that's too bad! Because if you manage your garden intelligently, the cup is almost never less than half full. My tomatoes were a complete washout in the frigid rains of 2009, but my broccoli was exceptionally gorgeous and delicious. CR raves, "My Brussels sprouts were amazing. I've never in 40 years seen stands of these vegetables that were so perfect." These are cool-loving crops that had no problem with our Siberian summer.

In another part of the country, an equivalent but opposite disaster yielded similar cup-half-full results. Ask Stephanie Van

Parys about the terrible drought Atlanta experienced in 2007, with severe restrictions on water use, and you can hear the shrug through the phone. "With crops like peppers and eggplants, the drier it gets, the better they perform. I had the best tomatoes ever." Stephanie is a horticulturist and the executive director of the Oakhurst Community Garden in the city of Decatur, Georgia, which is next to Atlanta. She is also a serious backyard vegetable grower, with an enormous 50- by 100-foot garden.

In this chapter, I want to talk about the strange nature of mastery in the vegetable garden, where even after 40 years, in the short run, you never know; where limited failure is part of the game, but time does teach the gardener how to minimize the risk of total failure; where even a terrible year yields so much beautiful food that complaints tend to be only half-serious.

Ask longtime gardeners what they do to ensure their own success, and you tend to hear the same few ideas over and over, though the methods they use to enact those ideas can be completely different: First, take care of the context in which it all happens, the soil. Second, diversify to avoid disaster. Third, pay attention to timing. And fourth, be a little Zen.

We've already talked about the first idea, enriching the soil with organic matter and keeping it covered with mulch. Stephanie Van Parys uses cover crops extensively, growing her own mulch. I use my alpaca bedding and leaves. Other gardeners rave about wood chips. The important point here is that mulch is a kind of insurance. It mitigates the effects of weird weather on the plants.

Next, experienced gardeners diversify for the same reason investors do: to spread the risk. Grow a big range of crops and something will always do well. Even better, plant a few varieties of every crop you really care about. Stephanie, who clearly has room to spare in her 5,000-square-foot garden, explains, "With tomatoes, I'll do 10 different varieties. With eggplants, I'll do 4 or 5. That way, I know that whatever the weather is like, some variety will be able to handle it."

While you can generalize about vegetable crops—peas want cool weather, beans like it warm—different varieties of the same vegetable can have very different tolerances. The seedlings of my favorite eggplant variety, 'Rosa Bianca', for example, wasted away in the cold, wet rains of 2009. However, the seedlings of an unnamed long black variety I picked up at a local nursery—clearly less bothered by low temperatures—managed to save me from being entirely eggplant free.

It is also possible to make the hardiest varieties in your particular growing conditions even hardier by saving their seeds. This only works with open-pollinated varieties, in other words, varieties that have been created over time by farmers and gardeners saving the seeds from those particular plants in a field that prove the toughest, most beautiful, unusual, or flavorful. (Most heirloom varieties fall into this category.) In turn, by saving seed from those plants in *your* garden that prove the toughest, most beautiful, unusual, or flavorful, you can encourage that variety to adapt even more completely to your own growing conditions.

Why doesn't this work with hybrids? Well, hybrids are not plants whose fine qualities are the product of incremental improvements over many generations. Hybrids are bred in one go, from the deliberate crossing of two unlike varieties, in hopes of getting the best qualities of both. In case you've forgotten your Gregor Mendel from high school biology—he was the Austrian abbot who, fooling around with peas, unlocked many of the secrets of genetics—hybrids are reliable only in their first generation, when the dominant traits of both parents prevail. Cross two hybrid plants and they reveal the true genetic grab bag of their origins. Many of their offspring will show disastrously undesirable recessive traits.

Open-pollinated varieties, on the other hand, are usually the product of like breeding with like, so they are genetically diverse within a much more narrow range and come more reliably "true" from seed. As a result, you can use the usually minor variations within the variety to improve what's already excellent.

Of course, it's not practical to save seeds from every open-pollinated vegetable unless you are ignoring your broker's advice to diversify and are planting just one variety of each, since some of them crossbreed too easily. The cucurbit family, for example, of squashes, pumpkins, cucumbers, and melons are notoriously promiscuous crossbreeders. One species, *Cucurbita pepo,* includes such different players as summer squashes, which taste good harvested small and unripe, and winter squashes and pumpkins, which don't. All of these will cross with each other unless separated by some substantial fraction of a mile. And lest you think that a pumpkin-zucchini hybrid sounds delicious—well, maybe one in a large number of such crosses might be. I've allowed the mongrel squash plants that appear in my compost to grow out a few times in the name of science. Their fruits had the taste and texture of a truck tire. No thanks.

Pepper varieties, too, will cross if not separated by at least 50 feet, and some people recommend 500. So if you grow hot and sweet peppers in the same bed, they can yield something that may look like a sweet pepper but carries a south-of-the-border kick.

On the other hand, it's easy to save lettuce, bean, tomato, and pea seeds, since the plants are largely self-pollinating. I routinely save pea and bean seeds, but just to avoid the irritating possibility that the seed companies will run out of my favorites before I place my order, not because I'm seriously trying to produce a better soup pea. Last year, one notably large and stately broccoli plant, towering above the bit players like John Wayne in a John Ford movie, tempted me towards Darwinian experiments. Yet I somehow preferred to eat the florets rather than let them go to seed. Possibly this explains why I am a writer and not a scientist. I'd want to sauté all the samples.

Another means of diversifying to avoid trouble in the vegetable garden is to rotate your crops. Moving things around from year to year befuddles pests and diseases and helps to avoid the soil depletion that can occur when similar crops requiring similar nutrients grow over and over in the same soil.

To rotate crops, group them into families when you plant them and make sure a few years pass before the same soil is used for the same family again. The key players here are the brassica family of cabbages, turnips, and broccoli; the nightshade family of tomatoes, eggplants, peppers, and potatoes; the legume family of peas and beans; and the cucurbit family of melons, squashes, cucumbers, and pumpkins that I just mentioned.

There are sophisticated methods of crop rotation that take into account the varying nutritional needs of these families, for example, by making sure that legumes, which fix nitrogen, are followed by brassicas, which want a lot of nitrogen. And these rotations are about to become a lot more sophisticated, Cornell University soil ecologist David Wolfe tells me, as more is learned about the ways different plants alter the soil through their root exudates. "We're at the frontier of understanding the legacy effects of different plants," he says.

Many market farmers employ spreadsheets in order to organize their crop rotations. But crop rotation can actually be more difficult in a home garden, where you are generally growing a large number of different vegetables in a limited space and by no means allotting the same amount of space to each family.

In a home garden, it also makes sense to maximize this limited space by succession planting—in other words, yanking the spring crops that poop out in the heat of summer, such as peas and radishes and a first planting of lettuces and potatoes, and then replacing them with hardy, fast-maturing crops that can be harvested in fall. These include lots of beautiful brassicas like turnips and kale, as well as lettuces, carrots, and potatoes.

Succession planting clearly adds to the complexity of trying to allow several years to pass before planting any relative of something you've already planted in your beds. I have to confess, my mental hard drive simply doesn't have the memory for this program. I could keep records. But I have never once in my life wanted to put my shovel down so I could take notes on what said shovel was doing, and I don't expect to reform this late in the game.

So I try to make it easy on myself. My garden is divided into quadrants, one of which is largely given over to permanent crops like asparagus, rhubarb, and lowbush blueberries. In the other three, I group relatives together and try to just shift the beds clockwise every year. And I don't fret about tucking bits of things in here and there during the season as space opens up. Despite this relatively casual attitude, I've had very little trouble with pests and diseases . . . until late blight arrived in 2009.

But late blight is a good argument for crop rotation, since thus far, the pest that causes the disease, a water mold with a diabolically complex and weapon-filled genome, is not reproducing sexually in America, with spores that can survive on their own in frozen ground. Instead, it winters over only in living tissue. If you've cleaned up diseased crop residues from your garden in fall, that means it can winter over only in the volunteer potatoes that come up in spring from tubers missed during the previous year's potato harvest. So it makes sense to keep the current crop of potatoes as far away on the other side of the garden from any potential volunteers as possible.

Late blight is one of nature's monsters, an exception to the general rule that if the soil is healthy, a backyard garden won't have a lot of problems, and even organic farmers spray against it. I'm violently anti-spraying in my own garden, a complete nature-mimicking minimalist. But if I lose my tomatoes another year? I can't vouch for my own virtue. I'm still developing as a gardener.

Next on the list, when you ask experienced gardeners what's most important to their success, is a sense of timing.

Timing is obviously important in short-season places like those where CR and I garden. In the Northeast, spring generally feels like being shot out of a cannon, so abrupt is the transition from snow to summer. And when winter is rushing up towards you from the moment that you take flight, it's easy to miss your chance at long-season crops if you flub a single cue.

The members of the cucurbit family of melons and squashes will give you some sense of the challenges I face with a frost-free season that is often not much longer than 100 days. Cucurbits can be started from seed in the house to cheat the season a bit, but only a few weeks before it's time to plant them. While cucurbits send up a pair of really tough-looking cotyledons—the embryonic first leaves—from their good-sized seeds, they are nonetheless delicate plants. Most of them are vines, and you really don't want to keep them inside long enough that they start to vine out in the pot, begin clinging desperately to whatever support is available, and have to be forcibly ripped off each other or your lamps or motocross trophies before planting.

And even when these seedlings grow to just the right size on just the right date, according to the calendar, and the last frost is well past, pleasant weather still counts for a lot. Cucurbit seedlings just don't like being planted into cold, wet ground and will simply wither into the great nothingness rather than put up with such discomfort. Starting them by seeding them directly into the soil soon after the last frost date, so they can choose their own moment to appear, is often more successful for me. But then I am completely at the mercy of Persephone and her grumpy husband Hades. He can't become too impatient with her summer-long independence—and demand that she join him underground too early in fall—if the melons and butternuts are going to ripen before it gets cold.

While other warm-season crops are more forgiving, still, you'd better have extra seedlings on hand in my part of the world, in case a late frost wipes out your tomatoes and eggplants, as happened to me in 2009, thanks to a frost June 1. It's always a tightrope walk when the season is short.

So, while I am easygoing about many things in the garden, timing is not one of them. For the last two gardening seasons, I've been working with a lovely woman who recently moved to Saratoga Springs from San Francisco to make the school garden I mentioned in the last chapter. I've noticed that she has very little anxiety about what needs to take place when—a mild-climate attitude or maybe just a California attitude. On the other hand, I frequently find myself pounding my fist on a school desk and shouting, "We need to order seeds *now*! We need to start seedlings *now*! We need to get the peas in *now*!" Timing questions definitely bring out my Teutonic side.

I'm especially driven in spring. I try to plant the earliest crops as soon as the ground thaws and the snow retreats, generally in early to mid-April, but this late date means some crops just won't work for me. Fava beans, much as I love them over pasta with bacon and shallots, need a longer period before the heat arrives than I can give them in most years. I plant them anyway, when I'm in the mood, but I never expect to get more than a meal or two out of the row before the plants blacken up in early July as if singed by a blowtorch.

And I've always struggled with what the books say are reliable spring crops: beets and brassicas such as radishes, turnips, and broccoli raab. These crops are all sensitive to day length, and planted in my late spring as we barrel towards the summer solstice, they tend to go to seed as small plants rather than producing something you'd want for dinner. Even when they do produce as expected, they have an unpleasant woody texture.

So I plant them according to the bit of folklore Harry Truman invoked when, hoping to pass civil rights legislation and a national health care plan, he called Congress back to Washington in the summer of 1948 for the famous Turnip Day sessions: "On the twenty-fifth of July," went the old Missouri saying, "sow your turnips, wet or dry."

CR Lawn attributes difficult springs in recent years in the Northeast to climate change: "I've noticed that our springs have become less and less reliable, with deluges of rain. But fall is warming and becoming more reliable. So my strategy is to put more energy now into the midsummer crops for fall." Indeed, scientists confirm what CR Lawn has gathered just by keeping his eyes open: that the Northeast is experiencing more "high-precipitation events," that the trend is likely to continue, and that this is likely to make spring more difficult for Northeastern farmers.

But even in places like Altadena, north of Pasadena in Southern California—a place that a winter-hardened gardener like me is likely to sniff at as basically paradise—there are still timing challenges, not to mention psychological pressure on the gardener to achieve nirvana year-round in a place where it's actually possible. Garden writer and designer Sandy Gillis, who has been growing vegetables in an idyllic yard with a white picket fence and hedges of Iceberg roses and dwarf lemon trees for 2 decades, tells me, "We've had sleet, hail, and snow only three times in 20 years, but we do get crazy frosts. Three nights of frost just killed my lettuce seedlings. I had to start all over! Five dollars' worth of seeds wasted!" I know the feeling. The difference is, Sandy gets to employ this faux-exasperated tone in *January*, while I save it for early June.

Generally, the first things into the garden every year are peas and spinach. The last things out are Brussels sprouts and kale. In between, with some frost tolerance and a preference for cooler weather, are radishes, cabbages, broccoli, turnips, and most greens, including lettuces, arugula, collards, chards, dandelions, and tatsoi. And with next to no frost tolerance and an appetite for heat are the cucurbits, tomatoes, peppers, eggplants, green beans, basil, okra, sweet potatoes, and tomatillos.

No matter where you live, making a smooth transition between the cool-loving spring crops, the heat-loving summer crops, and the heat-to-cool-loving fall crops always requires finesse.

Sandy says that in Southern California, "The tricky thing is to let the winter garden go as long as possible. You can start planting the summer garden here in March, but the winter garden is still going then."

Stephanie Van Parys of Atlanta, another long-season area, agrees that an unhurried summer means the gardener should relax about replacing spring crops with summer crops. Stephanie finds conventional wisdom about planting in Atlanta pretty faulty. "Home Depot will put their tomato seedlings out March 15. But the idea that you should put your summer crops in by Easter is hogwash. We've had 25-degree weather the first week in April. At my job, spring is really intense. So I have definitely pushed the envelope and planted my tomatoes out as late as July 30th. Anytime between April 15th and July 30th will work. And tomatoes planted April 15th will be petering out by July 30th, so a second crop is possible."

You'll notice nobody mentions sticking to an elaborate chart of planting and harvesting times, especially not one written by somebody else. These gardeners understand that paying attention to what happens out the back door is what really matters. As long as you understand the basic preferences of a crop in terms of spring, summer, or fall planting—seed packages offer pretty good advice in this direction—the rest is about noticing what works—and if it doesn't, shifting your planting either way.

A sense of timing helps even in pest control. I figured out that the one insect that was ever threatening in my garden, the Colorado potato beetle, was best dealt with when the adults first appeared in spring, before they mated and laid their eggs. That's because the larvae are more numerous and hungrier than their parents, and therefore much more devastating to the potato plants, as well as softer, pinker, and rawer-looking, so much less pleasant for the gardener to pick off and squish. CR, who sees cucumber beetles in his garden, says that the years have even taught him the ideal time of day to pick them off. "I go out at 5:00 a.m. when the dew is heavy, because the bugs are sluggish then and offer no resistance. Do that three or four mornings in a row, and you can cut the population considerably."

On the other hand, a sense of timing also means knowing when to just throw in the towel. "My French filet beans were eaten to a nub by bean beetles," says Stephanie Van Parys. "I just don't plant those anymore. There are too many other wonderful things to plant."

Like longtime parents, longtime gardeners learn when to fret and when to shrug. You fuss about watering when your seedlings are toddlers with shallow root systems. After that? You'll get better results if you don't hover too much. Adds Sandy Gillis, "When we go on a family vacation, we have to find a dog sitter and get somebody to take care of the chickens. Plants don't require that kind of attention. You do have to pay some attention when your seedlings are first getting established. After that, just relax, for crying out loud!"

Unfortunately, Sandy Gillis has yet to write that vegetable gardening how-to titled *Relax, for Crying Out Loud*, because this is another principle you'll hear from longtime gardeners: You can't control everything and generally don't need to control everything, so be a little Zen about it.

But this is not something you'll hear from most of the people who make a living peddling gardening advice. Beginners are often driven into foolishly exhausting efforts—or encouraged to take any disappointment personally—because the experts like to pretend to have secret information. They also like to pretend that once *you* learn their information, failure is not even possible. But that's not gardening. That's witchcraft.

Indeed, as you might expect from any endeavor that involves channeling the planet's life force, there is considerable magic in gardening advice, voodoo, mysticism, and strokes of genius arrived at after nervous breakdowns.

For example, I really admire organic movement pioneer Masanobu Fukuoka's ideas. He not only decided to eschew chemicals on his rice farm in Japan, but he questioned other disruptive agricultural practices too, including tilling the soil and applying compost every year, and decided they weren't necessary. He called his methods no-work farming, and I'm a no-work gardener.

However, some form of breakdown certainly seems to have been the starting point for him. He was a young scientist working in the city of Yokohama in the late 1930s, recently out of the hospital after a bout of pneumonia and struggling with a depression he could not shake. "One night as I wandered," he writes, "I collapsed in exhaustion on a hill overlooking the harbor, finally dozing against the trunk of a large tree." At dawn, the mist disappeared and a large heron appeared, and Fukuoka realized that all human knowledge is worthless. "Everything that had possessed me, all the agonies, disappeared like dreams and illusions, and something one might call 'true nature' stood revealed."

Voilà. A farming guru is born.

Of course, for the ripeness of the revelations, nobody beats Rudolf Steiner, the jack-of-all-trades philosopher and spiritualist of the turn of the 20th century. Steiner's supreme confidence in his own occult visions enabled him to instruct his followers in everything from education to dance to sculpture to religion to the behavior of gnomes to agriculture, where he is the founder of the biodynamic school. To read Steiner's lectures on agriculture is to experience a sprightly and not unenjoyable form of cognitive dissonance. A PhD in philosophy, Steiner edited Goethe early in his career, and he retains the tone of a scholar while offering a witch doctor's advice.

To rid a field of mice, for example, he recommends, "First, catch a fairly young mouse and skin it. . . . We must burn the skin of the mouse when Venus is in the sign of the Scorpion and carefully collect the ash and anything left over. . . . We take the pepper we have made in this way and scatter it on our fields."

That's because when produced at precisely the right moment according to the Zodiac, this mouse pepper "contains the negative of the field mouse's reproductive force." Steiner doesn't specify whether this negative force is a form of birth control or merely repellent to the poor mice. But he assures us, "If everyone in the neighborhood does this, the results will certainly be dramatic."

Then, like the polished showman he must have been, Steiner ends this portion of his lecture with a little joke: "I venture to say we might develop a taste for such things and come to enjoy them. Farms, like certain foods, taste better with a little pepper!"

Amazingly enough, Steiner's agricultural revelations still have influence to this day, and his followers among gardening gurus are still pushing odd potions such as yarrow flowers fermented in a deer bladder, planting by the moon and stars, and doing companion planting based on what vegetable in theory "likes" what other vegetable.

But even a paranoid can have enemies, as Henry Kissinger famously remarked. And even crackpots can be right about certain questions. Steiner was right about some important things, including his conviction that chemical fertilizers were not adequate food for the living soil. And he had such a conviction early, before the process that allowed for the industrial production of artificial nitrogen was more than a few years old. His work is a mixed bag people are still digging into, because some of it made sense.

It's important for beginners to understand that most gardening schools—not just biodynamic, but also biointensive, lasagna, square foot, permaculture, and MiracleGro—are cults, down to their sometimes insinuating assumptions about the politics and life goals of their followers. These programs are not science. Their authors are not doing side-by-side field tests to determine whether you should be tilling your garden every year, or not tilling at all; or whether it's better to space your crops so closely that they shade the soil or whether it's better to mulch and give the plants room to grow; or whether raised beds are the answer to all life's problems or problematic in their free drainage.

So their advice is often contradictory—almost as contradictory as *actual* science, where you will still find one group of scientists who consider artificial fertilizers an inevitability and another who consider them an anathema.

I realize, however, that poor beginners long for some definitive advice that will keep them from embarrassing themselves in their first efforts and make their gardens foolproof.

To understand the extreme difficulty of formulating such advice, you need to talk to someone like Dr. Beth Medvecky of the Cornell International Institute for Food, Agriculture, and Development, an expert in low external-input agriculture, who spent 10 years doing adaptive research in western Kenya. Dr. Medvecky has been trying to help the hungry farmers there, mostly women, increase the productivity of small plots depleted by intensive planting and little or no fertilization. "Farmers can't afford a bag of fertilizer," Dr. Medvecky says, "in a place where laborers make just a dollar a day."

These farmers were most concerned about their inability to grow enough of the staple crop maize even to meet the demands of their households, so Dr. Medvecky worked on a number of alternative fertilization strategies with them to improve their yields. These included adding nitrogen to the soil by growing a drought-tolerant, nitrogen-fixing legume there in the dry season, when maize wouldn't grow. "We screened 30 different species of legumes," she tells me, "trying to see which ones could be productive occupying the land during the dry season. One legume, *Lablab purpureus,* produced an edible grain, and that was the one the farmers wanted."

By one measure, she was really successful. "Over 7 years, we developed strategies for farmers that helped them *quadruple* their maize production. But there were unintended consequences. Once the legumes were introduced, the farmers noticed that their beans, which they planted in the same row with the maize, began doing badly." Beetles, whose larvae spend the rainy season eating plant roots and then burrow deep into the soil in the dry season to pupate, were the culprits. Normally, when they emerge as adults, there is very little plant matter to eat other than the leaves of trees. But Dr. Medvecky and her dry-season legume were offering a meal at a critical moment, and she suspects that the beetles were now mating in the farm fields over this meal and laying their eggs there.

"This issue was not on our radar screen," she says, humbly. "The learning goes on." In other words, even for an expert like Dr. Medvecky, a good plan in the abstract can prove problematic in practice. "One size does not fit all," she emphasizes.

We need more science in gardening. In fact, we need a *lot* more of it to illuminate the important principles, which are still in dispute, and to rid the subject of its current excess of superstition, make-work, and fantasy. But I think it's highly unlikely that science will ever eliminate the mysteries of my particular plot of land and the gazillion creatures on and in it, to the point of offering me a road map.

As CR Lawn puts it, "If you try to think of gardening as a science, it doesn't work. There are too many variables. It's an art."

Well, artists take their inspiration from all kinds of places, so by all means adopt a principle or two from a cult that seems congenial to you! Try the lasagna or the raised beds, or the companion planting, or the planting by the cycles of the moon, or the stinky potions, or God forbid, if you are a masochist bored with hitting yourself in the head with a hammer, the double digging. But make sure you retain a bit of skepticism. Once the cult leaders start trying to convince you to stop cutting your hair and talking to your parents and to join a polygamous household, it might be time to put on the brakes.

If you garden for a few years, and keep your eyes and ears open, you will almost inevitably outgrow the cult's point of view, because you will understand something they don't: the very specific things communicated by your piece of earth.

Like artists, longtime gardeners hear their muses speak in a murmur beneath language. CR says that after 40 years, he has a good feeling for the weather patterns that affect the garden. "Sometimes, you just have a hunch about when to plant melons. I don't even know why I know. You get to the point where you watch the weather, study the clouds, look at the moon. I love it when I'm right and the weather forecaster is wrong!"

I can't say that I've grown sagacious about weather over my 2 decades in the garden. I'm still constantly shocked and outraged by its weirdness. But, as I mentioned in Chapter 5, I have had life-altering revelations about managing my soil. And years of trial and error have made me imagine that I understand what all kinds of crops "want," which is basically to be planted in good soil and timed correctly.

All of us longtime gardeners are guilty of experiencing our own irrational, unprovable revelations about what works in the garden. The difference between most of us and Rudolf Steiner is that we laugh at ourselves for feeling especially smart, because we've been out in the yard long enough to lose our melons to cold or basil to drought, and we know that arrogance is foolishness.

Gardening is never risk free. It's not risk free in your first year and it's not risk free in your 40th. And that is one of the very best things about having a vegetable garden. There's always another strange spin on the ball. There's always more to learn. The adventure is never done.

NINE

Survival

How to Stay Adaptable in Uncertain Times

If you are an avid newspaper reader, it's hard not to worry about the future of civilization. It's not just climate change, water shortages, or humanity's insatiable appetite for fuel. It's the fact that we will be more than 9 billion people on this planet by 2050, or so the United Nations projects. The planet is already plenty crowded as is. And I'm pretty sure that most of those 9 billion, being human, will be just like the 6.8 billion of us here today. They will want to use as much of everything as possible—oil, water, land, food—as immediately as possible, and only fret about the consequences when they are pounding at the door.

But, if you live in my house, it's *really* hard not to worry about the future. My husband, the most optimistic and confident man I know, has been on the climate change beat as a reporter for the last 10 years and has written two books about it. So dinner-table conversation tends to involve 15-foot sea-level rises, London and New Orleans underwater, hundreds of millions of climate refugees, the possibility of mass starvation, and a vicious cycle set off by melting permafrost that will release trapped stores of the superpotent greenhouse gas methane. Now, pass the Parmesan!

We also happen to live in the same town as James Howard Kunstler, a famous dystopian and author of many books, including recently *The Long Emergency,* which is about dwindling oil reserves and the coming end of what he calls the "cheap oil fiesta" of American civilization. Jim Kunstler, who possesses loads of elfin charm despite the dire prognostications, is an extremely kind and amusing friend, a terrific host, great cook, big gardener, and life-lover in general. But again, his assumption is that a comfortable person like myself is in for a very bumpy ride at some point not too far down the road.

Fortunately, we gardeners tend to take a calm view of all disaster scenarios, because we're at least equipped to feed ourselves. I'd be willing to bet, in fact, that there is no serious vegetable gardener without a little vanity on the score of doomsday. I grow so much beautiful food in the few hours a week I give to the endeavor that I tell myself that I could scale up the operation rapidly, if necessity demanded.

But there is an essential difference between amateur gardeners like me and professional farmers—let alone do-it-themselves survivalists. In a hobby garden, no one suffers long if the turnips prove to be woody or if there's an unfortunate lull between the early crops and the crops of high summer. Miscalculations, omissions, and accidents of God do not lead to hunger.

So if one of my crops fails, I shrug. If I don't feel like planting something, I don't.

I have a sense of what becoming truly self-sufficient would

entail. I am constantly pushing *towards* self-sufficiency because I find that my own sourdough bread is *so* much better than the bakery's, and the eggs from my own three hens *so* much better even than those from the farmers' market, and my own sauerkraut, too, *so* much better than the stuff in jars at the supermarket. And interestingly enough, so far every step forward on the road to self-sufficiency saves me time, by saving me a fraction of a shopping trip every month. Next on the list for me is setting up a passive solar greenhouse for winter salads in my city yard and maybe talking my city neighbor into going halfsies with me on a pair of milking goats so we can make cheese.

I'm always moving deeper into the food frontier and probably will be until I'm dead. But, barring apocalypse, I don't think I need to actually *reach* that destination called self-sufficiency.

Right now, I generate a flood of fresh food casually, in the dregs of my time. But to grow and freeze and dry and can enough food to last my family of five the entire year long . . . to plan for a year's worth of meals, and of sufficient variety and quality to avoid mutiny in February . . . to find a wheat variety that works in my part of the world and grow it and mill it . . . to make juices to replace the Tropicana . . . to milk a cow twice a day . . . and to do it all without any help or interest from anybody else in the household . . . well, let's just say that I am aware of the concept of diminishing returns. To do all that stuff right, I'm assuming I'd have to either quit the day job or give the children away to relatives.

I point this out because I think it's important for beginning gardeners not to allow ambitions born of ignorance to ruin their enjoyment. The clearest example I can think of involves my lifelong best friend Donna and the analogous subject of cooking. Donna began dating her husband Leo, the president of the company where she worked—a big, wise, authoritative, self-made man who is 25 years older than she is—when she was 24. She and Leo have run a series of businesses ever since, and the money for a nice restaurant meal has never been a problem, so Donna never learned to cook. But one day Donna got it into her head that she would take up cooking. Did she go out and buy a few nice knives and a good ethnic cookbook with delicious foolproof recipes? This is what I would have recommended, if she'd asked.

Nope. She spent hundreds of dollars on a grain mill.

See, she'd decided that if she was going to cook, she was going to make bread, and if she was going to make bread, she'd grind her own flour. Needless to say, Donna does not now cook.

The gardening equivalent of Donna might be journalist Manny Howard, who produced a cover story in *New York Magazine* and a book called *My Empire of Dirt* out of his attempt, over one growing season, with no knowledge or experience whatsoever, to feed himself from his Brooklyn backyard. Howard claimed that this was some kind of investigation of the furthest implications of the locavore movement. But let's call it the other thing he openly admits it was: a stunt.

This stunt revealed nothing that I can identify about eating locally and very little about growing your own food, except that if you try to do the hardest thing right off the bat—grow *all* your own food on a tiny plot of land—with no preparation or research, you'll probably botch a lot of things up. Howard wasted lots of money and time on digging a drainage system in his backyard and trucking in tons of soil, when an experienced gardener probably would have dealt with the same problems by slapping together a few raised beds—and gotten the spring crops in on time.

And he blundered from gardening—easy and rewarding—into animal husbandry—which is another deal entirely. Howard laid in rabbits, chickens, and ducks, and the results were not pretty. "The rabbits," he writes, "kept themselves cool in the summer heat by kicking over their water dishes. The wet conditions invited flies to lay eggs, which turned into maggots, which attached themselves to the does. I lost a doe and the kids' buck to hideous infestations that I care not to describe further or ever think of again."

Animals! These are not for fools.

Even the author of the back-to-the-lander's Bible, John Seymour of *The Complete Book of Self-Sufficiency,* urged some caution. Seymour's 35-year-old book is a complete source of fascination and delight for anybody with do-it-yourself tendencies—it will tell you how to make bricks and beer, as well as how to grow raspberries—but in the foreword to the most recent edition, Seymour wrote, "I would offer this advice: Do not try to do everything at once. This is an organic way of life, and organic processes tend to be slow and steady."

Right. If you look at your own development as a gardener as an organic process, one where your ambitions grow as your experience does, you will be astonished at your powers.

El Parcels, who writes a charming and super-literate blog called *Fast Grow the Weeds* about her own homesteading adventures on 5 acres in southern Michigan, suggests that there's even something addicting about those powers. "My first homegrown tomato was like a gateway drug," she laughs. "Even when I was a city person, I was growing tomatoes, but it wasn't enough."

Like me, El has a job and maternal duties—she is an architect with a 6-year-old daughter. Yet her ambitions on the food front have ramped up over the 5 years she's owned her small farm to the point that she produces almost everything her family eats, except for beef, cow's milk, and wheat. "My refrigerator is almost empty," she says. In other words, dinner is fetched, not shopped for. To say that El was not born to the life of a subsistence farmer is an understatement. "I did a little genealogical research at some point," she tells me. "I am *six* generations away from anyone who's done this." She also mentions having been a painted-fingernails kind of person in her youth.

Nonetheless, besides her vegetable garden, she has poultry for meat and eggs, a milking goat, and two enormous greenhouses for produce in the winter and spring. "The first year I put up a greenhouse, I went out there in January, and it was so wonderful, I instantly thought," she laughs, "'I need to get a second one!' It's more, more, more!" She dries beans, she cans, she makes cheese. Then there are those projects that only a total foodie after my own heart would take on. She is building a wood-fired outdoor oven and hopes to make an entirely homegrown pizza in it next season— which means growing the wheat for the flour. Oh yeah, she grows so many grapes, she's going to try her hand at wine this fall, too.

Ask her how she's able to keep expanding her empire and she says, "Well, I don't watch TV. And every year, as I add something new, I economize with my time in other ways. You realize, oh, the garden needs constant weeding. It would be easier to mulch instead."

El's husband is an artist, not one of nature's gentlemen farm-ers, but he has good-naturedly assisted El in her empire building. "He's basically gone along with my schemes," she says. "But by now, it's clear that I'm not crazy! The proof is on the plate!"

There is no denying the joy in El's voice as she describes her culinary queendom. But if you ask my friend Erich Kranz about the experiment in self-sufficiency he and his first wife conducted in their late twenties, you will elicit a long, anguished groan. They tried raising almost all their own food on 3 acres as, he explains, "rehearsal for getting off the grid and retiring."

Rick is an MIT-educated chemical engineer and was work-ing in Boston at the time. His goal was to spend 3 years learning how to homestead, and then exit the rat race early by buying a farm in the ski country of New Hampshire, where he and his wife would support themselves by the sweat of their brows and by sell-ing a bit of meat to fancy ski-resort restaurants. "But the rehearsal for retirement was a flop," Rick laughs. He couldn't make the economics of raising meat on a small scale work, despite the exhausting amount of labor he donated to his livestock after a long day at the office. He sighs, "It became apparent that we had to have *jobs* to be able to live off the grid." This, of course, defeated the entire idea. He does change tone for a moment as he adds, "The vegetable garden, on the other hand, was wonderful." The economics of *that* worked.

Today, more than 30 years later, Rick is married to my lovely friend Martha Culliton, the cookbook writer and scholar of food I mentioned earlier, a woman who makes her own paprika from her own peppers. They live on 80 acres in a house he built just up the road from me in the county. Rick is once again raising barns and animals, and in his early sixties, is a compact, tanned, and handsome argument for getting out of the office and into a field. In fact, he raises most of the meat I buy. The difference is that now he really *is* retired, so he has the time to spend farming and no longer really cares about the economics. "I'm doing it because our food supply has gone to hell," he says. "These constant recalls of beef, for example, are pretty scary. Plus our own meat tastes incredible." In other words, he is providing the kind of ingredients his wife the genius cook deserves.

As my country neighbor, Rick is my ace in the hole come the apocalypse. I know how to grow food crops. Rick knows how to wire, plumb, construct, fix broken machinery, and raise an excellent ham. Martha will make sure that our little band of neighbors and friends is not cooking gruel over a fire, but dining beautifully. There is also our neighbor Herb, who raises the alpacas whose fleece his wife Faith spins into gorgeous wool, so if we are huddled around a fire, we'll at least be wearing chic sweaters. I even have a rocky southeast-facing slope that looks perfect for Gewürztraminer grapes. On our road in Salem, New York, doomsday doesn't look so bad . . . though, every time I spin out such a scenario, my husband annoys me by mentioning desperate climate refugees raiding my fields. Or he brings up Cormac McCarthy's harrowing little novel *The Road,* in which apocalypse takes the form of a nuclear winter–like environmental disaster in which nothing grows—not even those relatively hardy Alsatian grapes used for my favorite white wines.

No Gewürztraminer? Maybe I'm not cut out for survivalism after all.

My own sense about producing food is that it is a lark—until necessity enters into it. Once life and limb, or even just livelihood, depends on the success of your crops, everything changes.

Aaren Hatalsky, a young farmer who lives in the country-side near Saratoga Springs, is particularly articulate on the transition between gardener and farmer, because it's one that she has made only in the last few years. She is one of a rising new breed of farmers that is altering the USDA statistics: female, college-educated, and farming a small piece of land diversely, intensively, and sustainably. She is also as smart as a whip and totally adorable, with a heart-shaped face and brilliant white teeth peeking out from behind tortoiseshell glasses and a curtain of corkscrew-curly brown hair.

"I had my own little garden from 10 years old on," she tells me. "Picking something for dinner was always part of my life. At 18 or 19, I became interested in homesteading and survivalism, in part because I wanted to travel and wanted to know my way around the woods and the wilderness."

She was working behind a desk at a nonprofit after college when a friend told her he'd just gotten an organic farming internship. Her jealousy was so intense, it was clearly love revealed, the plot of every Hollywood romcom since time immemorial, only it was farming that she wanted. Today, Aaren and her boyfriend Chris, a software engineer, are in the process of buying the lovely spot she's farmed for the last two seasons: 10 quiet acres and a Victorian farmhouse of such simple, stately calm that I had a terrible attack of house envy in her farmhouse kitchen. While she does some sales at farmers' markets, her basic model is CSA, or community supported agriculture: Her customers buy shares in the farm's produce ahead of time and, in return, receive vegetables and eggs every week from May to October.

She describes the learning curve she's been on in moving from gardener to farmer as "cramming." She works all day—and then spends her evenings reading furiously.

"On top of the basic requirements of the crops, I had to learn greenhouse plant etiquette, which is tricky," she tells me. "I had to learn about cultivation and weed control. If you think about it, in a garden, you are never on the soil with heavy equipment. A load of compost covers the whole thing. You can weed by hand and mulch with a wheelbarrow. It's entirely different on a farm. I also had to learn about new tools, washing the produce, cooling, storage—some things like to be in plastic and some things don't. Disease and pest control become an issue that they are not in a garden; I can now identify about 40 different things that can go wrong. Farmers are glued to the weather service, too, because one strange weather event can wipe you out."

The biggest trick psychologically, according to Aaren, is knowing when to stop. "My home and my job are the same place. There's no window I can look out of without seeing something that has to be done. You have to make lists or you wind up wandering aimlessly around the property finding things to do. You're always behind. Plus, the place always has to look good. When my CSA members come here, they want to see something charming, not dangerous shards of metal sticking out of the ground."

As a result, she sighs, "You have to give up on things that used to be important pastimes like traveling. I can see that old farmers get crusty and resentful because they can never leave their places. They become distant from the rest of humanity."

She adds, in a slightly plaintive tone, "I'm trying to hang on to my life."

Okay, farming isn't easy. So it's important to remember what Aaren is accomplishing. On just an acre and a quarter of cultivated land, she is producing enough vegetables to feed 30 *families* half the year, and she is building her soil while she's doing it, not exhausting it the way an industrial farm would.

Of course, there are many people who would argue that the efforts of small farmers like Aaren, vegetable gardeners like me, and self-sufficient types like El are meaningless in a crowded world.

There are many distinguished scientists who say that the world can't step backwards from industrial farming, no matter how disastrous it is environmentally, because it's the only way to feed the earth's giant population. Energy expert Vaclav Smil has pointed out that the Haber-Bosch synthesis—in other words, the industrial process that generates artificial nitrogen fertilizer—"now provides the very means of survival for about 40 percent of humanity."

Then there is Nobel Prize winner Norman Borlaug, often called the father of the Green Revolution for his work on high-yield grains that rapidly increased food production in Asia in the 1960s. Before his death in 2009, he more than once offered a stinging rebuke to critics of factory farming that they just didn't understand hunger. For example, in a 2000 lecture, he said, "We cannot lose sight of the enormous job before us to feed 10 to 11 billion people. . . . While the affluent nations can certainly afford to adopt ultra low-risk positions and pay more for food produced by the so-called 'organic' methods, the 1 billion chronically undernourished people of the low-income, food deficit nations cannot."

In other words, the future of food on a crowded planet is more technology, not less, and bringing industrial methods to people who don't yet have them: genetically engineered seeds, synthetic fertilizers, and tractors. More of the same, plus possibly finding new ways to avoid the fragile soil entirely, by growing artificial muscle in vats for meat and vegetables in 10-story hydroponic greenhouses.

On the other hand, in 2008, the United Nations Environment Programme looked at hundreds of farming projects in Africa, where small farmers have not had access to all the tools of modern food production, and found that organic systems more than doubled crop yields.

I am well aware that given the scale of the problem of feeding all of humanity, there is some absurdity in even discussing what I am doing. But we backyard gardeners do prove that in relatively favorable climates, it's possible to produce enough food for ourselves and a few others, without a lot of land and without a lot of collateral damage. So I am extremely impatient with the charge I often hear that the rise of small-scale local growers and backyard gardeners in America is nothing but a sentimental fantasy. The *Freakonomics* blog at the *New York Times* Web site, for example, seems to relish bashing locavores and gardeners.

Stephen J. Dubner, the journalist half of the team behind the best-selling *Freakonomics* books, attacks the very idea of gardening on the grounds that it's less efficient in economic, environmental, and even culinary terms than leaving the farming to professionals: "Specialization is ruthlessly efficient. Which means less transportation, lower prices—and, in most cases, far more *variety,* which in my book means more deliciousness and more nutrition." Clearly, Dubner has *no idea* what deliciousness really is, if he doesn't understand that a backyard garden is the Saudi Arabia of deliciousness.

But it's worth considering Dubner's assumption that the backyard garden is less efficient as a food source than the giant industrial farm. Are we small family-feed operations really doing nothing of any value to anyone? Is my vision of the future—a billion sustainable backyard gardens and small farms—really more ridiculous than a vision of a future in which all the growing of food is done by industry—or does mine just seem ridiculous because it's prettier?

First of all, if it's not sustainable—and industrial agriculture as practiced today is most definitely not—its efficiency won't matter in the long term.

Second, food is just different from other products, in that it requires the cooperation of nature, rather than the cooperation of factory owners in China. There are actually some *dis*economies of scale in agriculture, given that scale means a disease-prone, pest-prone, soil-exhausting, oil-guzzling, machine-accommodating monoculture.

Around the world, scientists have long noticed an inverse relationship between the size of a farm and its productivity. Even in the United States, the USDA's agricultural census shows that the smallest farms beat the pants off the biggest farms in terms of sales of agricultural goods per acre. A big farm is generally able to produce a single crop more efficiently than a small farm. However, on a small farm, diverse crops are often planted sequentially and intensively to make the best possible use of a plot throughout the growing season, and the farmer is actually out there with his or her feet in the dirt, raising the total output per unit of land just by paying attention. And I would bet that kitchen gardens, where the greedy gardener has crammed arugula and cilantro onto every last inch of soil, represent the most efficient use of land of all.

A kitchen garden is also more efficient in that it requires far fewer inputs per potato. The problems large-scale growers feel they have to combat with chemical fertilizers, herbicides, and pesticides often never even rear their heads in a backyard garden. And the only energy input that's required by the vegetable garden is the caloric energy contributed by the gardener.

Yes, admittedly, industrial farms win the efficiency battle on one front: labor costs. One bored guy sitting in a piece of equipment the size of a house can work many, many acres of conventionally farmed land all planted in one crop, whereas Aaren is exhausting herself working just a single diversely planted acre. On the other hand, young, college-educated small farmers like Aaren clearly have choices and still choose to farm. Obviously, it's a rewarding profession, and maybe it wouldn't be so bad if our economy produced a lot more farmers. The food might cost more, but we'd get greater value for our money. And as for home gardeners, well, the labor we expend merely makes us fit, and no gym time required. Highly efficient!

In fact, I'd argue that the food-loving backyard gardeners, the doughty self-sufficient types, and the intrepid small farmers are actually increasing the efficiency of the entire food system by bringing wasted land online again. One of the greatest worries about a growing population is that while the demand for food is growing right along with it, the supply of arable land isn't. But clearly, an industrial definition of *arable* doesn't take into account the vast acreage we squander in our American yards. For the first time last season, my next-door neighbor in Saratoga Springs turned a city backyard—every inch of it aside from a deck for dining—into a source of food. While all the people I've mentioned in this chapter—Aaren, El, Rick and Martha, and me—are growing food on what was farmland, most of our places were abandoned by farmers long ago. We've carved our spots out of weeds, brush, and sumac.

Of course, the Freakonomics guys and Manny Howard would argue that my little band of foodies would be far more productive for society as a whole if we spent more time at our desks plying our actual professions, rather than out in our vegetable beds.

After his own misadventures in the world of food production, Howard arrives at this gentle conclusion: "Our bountiful era is predicated on the division of labor: We don't sew our own clothes, we don't build our own houses—and we certainly don't farm—because we're too busy doing whatever it is we do for everyone else."

Putting aside the self-congratulatory nature of the argument, is extreme specialization *really* the ideal way to organize human society? Is it really good for all of us to be utterly powerless outside our own areas of professional expertise?

It's possible to see that ideal of specialization fully realized in the America of the early 21st century. There are many people in every American city and town who would no sooner pick up a hammer or a shovel or spatula than they would fly to the moon, and there are umpteen businesses happy to compensate for their unwillingness to use their hands: to feed, house, transport, climate-control, groom, and amuse them, all for a modest fee. As a young Manhattanite, I was well on my way to becoming just such a dependent person, I fear, until my garden helped me discover my own powers.

The problem with a society of such super-specialists is that it is not adaptable, if our bountiful era should abruptly become less bountiful and practical skills are suddenly required. One of Jim Kunstler's prognostications in *The Long Emergency* is that once there is any kind of disruption in our supply of cheap fuel, "Producing food will become a problem of supreme urgency." Who knows, really, what shocks we may be in for in the coming years, thanks to our extreme dependence on fossil fuels, climate change, the possibility of a flu pandemic, and all the economic dislocations of recent years? At a minimum, adaptability is a great quality in times of radical change.

But even if we Americans continue to be comfortable for many decades to come, there is another reason to learn some practical skills like making a garden: because these skills make you a bigger, smarter, shrewder, more *worldly* person—and that is likely to make you better at every single thing you do, including conducting an audit or writing a marketing plan.

One of science fiction writer Robert Heinlein's characters expresses this idea beautifully: "A human being should be able to change a diaper, plan an invasion, butcher a hog, conn a ship, design a building, write a sonnet, balance accounts, build a wall, set a bone, comfort the dying, take orders, give orders, cooperate, act alone, solve equations, analyze a new problem, pitch manure, program a computer, cook a tasty meal, fight efficiently, die gallantly.

"Specialization," he concludes, "is for insects."

Personally, I like knowing how to do stuff, especially how to grow beans and cook them beautifully. These activities are extremely enjoyable and so meaningful to me that I would no more outsource them than I'd outsource the raising of my children. They connect me with the whole of human history, which, let's face it, has been largely about scrambling to find the next meal.

Such primitive knowledge gives me a certain confidence that if our cushy civilization should ever fail me, I am ready for anything.

Undoubtedly, this readiness is an illusion. But let's just say that we backyard gardeners are *readier* than people who consider themselves too highly evolved to shake a packet of seeds over the ground.

TEN

Happiness

The Best Reason to Garden

The first time I ever held a shovel, I didn't know how to use it. It was early spring, and I was trying to break up the rocky ground in my backyard with arm strength alone. I'd plunge the point of the shovel towards the sod, and it would just slide off the surface.

My husband, once he got done laughing at me, was gracious enough to show me how to stomp on a shovel to make it effective. As soon as that first bit of soil yielded to my boot, I instantly thought, "I like this."

I was still thinking, "I like this" 3 hours later, when my 90-year-old neighbor, a retired farmer named Freemont, came over to check on my progress. He looked at the absurd 2½-foot-deep trench I'd dug out of ignorance, rolled his eyes, and barked, "Where are you planting that stuff, *China*?"

Twenty years later, I never step into the garden without thinking, "I like this." I like it so much that I can hardly wait every year for winter to turn into spring, so I can set up a bamboo trellis for my peas and toss a handful of spinach seed over the ground and start the cycle of life spinning on my piece of earth once more.

The peas and spinach will be delicious enough by themselves to leave any gardener aglow. But the vegetable garden is as much about the experience as the food, and the experience is simply one of life's most beautiful.

The smell of good soil, the exercise of digging, the beauty of the plants, the sound of the birds, the feeling of the sun on your face, the sense of accomplishment and power—these things are entirely irresistible. While I garden for a million fine reasons, underlying them all is the fact that I never feel more optimistic, engaged, productive, or peaceful than when I am in my garden.

The garden is simple for me, in that it is simply wonderful, but the happiness it offers is a 10-ply kind of happiness, one made up of animal exhilaration as well as more philosophical satisfactions. I'd like to end this book by pulling apart those strands and considering why something as mundane as a vegetable garden can be such a source of meaning and joy.

First of all, there is something about the soil that may be literally *something.* Some of the mud bugs immunologist Graham Rook talked about in Chapter 5 seem not only to regulate the immune system, but also mood. A trial of lung cancer patients found that when they were given the soil bacteria *Mycobacterium vaccae,* their survival time did not improve, but their quality of life did, unexpectedly. They felt better, physically and emotionally.

Inspired by these findings, University of Colorado at Boulder neuroscientist Christopher Lowry has done experiments using the same dirt bug in mice. "We found that it has antidepressant-like effects . . . not that the mice we were studying were depressed," he laughs. "But we know how mice given Prozac behave."

If turns out that if you give a mouse Prozac and throw it into a pool of water, it will swim much longer before giving up on trying to escape and passively floating than an ordinary mouse. The same is true of mice injected with soil bacteria: They will fight an unpleasant fate much longer. "It's a proactive type of coping," Dr. Lowry explains.

He adds, "It's very novel. The bacteria seems to activate a small group of serotonin neurons involved in cognitive function and moods." The results were so promising that Dr. Lowry is now working with a group of psychiatrists to set up clinical trials to see if this bacteria can be used to treat depressed people.

Interestingly enough, Dr. Lowry has also found that the same areas of the brain that appear to be activated by the dirt bug are also activated by warm temperatures, which may explain why exercise, which raises our body temperatures, is so cheering—and why the sweaty business of working with a shovel in the summer sunshine makes me so happy.

While scientists like Dr. Lowry are just beginning to tease out the changes in the brain caused by exercise that explain why it is so effective in reducing stress, there is almost universal agreement that it does reduce stress, elevate mood, increase confidence, and make optimists out of pessimists. It's certainly essential to me.

In fact, I look back on my early life with a certain disbelief at its lazy lack of physicality. I did nothing but read as a kid. Even into my early thirties, my interests were largely cultural. But I have not grown more scholarly as I've aged. Now, at 50, I find myself with the appetites of your average Greek shipping tycoon. What do I want out of life? Sex, beautiful food, wine, laughs with the tribe, and exhilarating labor out of doors. And my vegetable garden yields or encourages a bunch of the above.

Even the plants themselves may be contributing to my expansive mood in the garden. Medical professionals dating back to ancient Egypt have long understood that contact with plants makes people relax and feel better. Research has shown that even looking out a window at greenery makes people in grim circumstances—hospitals, public housing, prisons—happier. Today, institutions of all kinds from hospitals to programs for troubled teenagers use gardens and farms specifically designed to be therapeutic. Nancy Chambers, the longtime head of New York City's Rusk Institute of Rehabilitation Medicine's garden, told me she has noticed that when patients are in the garden, they seem to forget all about their pain, and their pain medication.

Why do plants make us feel better? Evolutionary biologists say that we are programmed to relax around food crops, because they obviously mean that nobody's starving tonight. And who knows? Given plants' incredible facility at producing chemicals to further their ends—including luring in pollinators by mimicking the pollinators' sex hormones—it's possible that the vegetables are actually dosing us in the garden, giving off chemicals that influence our health and mood for the better, so we'll keep planting their seeds.

Of course, most of these mood influencers—the soil bugs, the sunshine, the contact with plants—could be obtained passively. A walk in a botanical garden or a visit to a farm might do the job. Gardening, however, is not a passive activity. It is something you have to choose to throw yourself into, and the happiness it offers is cerebral and emotional as well as physical.

In my case, I find that my cares just drop away in the garden, and the hours I spend there pass like minutes. Even when my gardening day is spent on my back in a ditch, miserably nailing cage wire to a fence, I never feel that my time is wasted. I always emerge before dinner with the sense that I am slightly richer in the kind of elemental knowledge that runs deeper than language and reason, and I understand something new about the earth's diurnal course or the locomotion of worms.

While there has been much written on the subject of happiness from the ancient philosophers on, the description of happiness that best matches my own experience of that emotion is found in the work of Mihaly Csikszentmihalyi, the psychologist who is one of the fathers of the positive psychology movement of recent years. In his wise and beautiful book *Flow: The Psychology of Optimal Experience*, Csikszentmihalyi sums up decades of research across many cultures into what makes people happy with the word *flow*.

Flow experiences, which can include everything from playing volleyball to working out a mathematical proof, have a few defining characteristics that seem to make them universally enjoyable. They offer a challenge that engages but doesn't overwhelm your skills. The challenge is so absorbing that you lose all sense of time, lose any self-consciousness and the sense of being separate from the activity you're pursuing. At a moment of flow, the dance and the dancer become one, and the same goes for the mountain and the mountaineer, as well as the garden and the gardener.

According to Csikszentmihalyi, it is because of our limitations as human beings that we have such flow experiences. Our central nervous systems can process only a few pieces of information at a time. So when our mind is fully engaged in a challenging task, there is no room for mundane worries, bad memories, beating oneself up, ambivalence, boredom, or annoyance at the grinding sound of the neighbor's lawn mower.

And thank goodness! If we could respond to every thought and sensation simultaneously, we'd be pecked to death by regret, resentment, and fear.

Csikszentmihalyi explains, "Being able to forget temporarily who we are seems to be very enjoyable. When we are not preoccupied with our selves, we actually have a chance to expand the concept of who we are. Loss of self-consciousness can lead to self-transcendence, to a feeling that the boundaries of our being have been pushed forward."

And that's the difference between the flow experience called gardening and your average tranquilizer. A bottle of wine might help you forget yourself, too, but you'll come out of the experience with nothing but a hangover. A sunny Saturday spent in the vegetable garden, on the other hand, offers you a chance to see beyond the end of your nose into an endless frontier and to grow by embracing it.

To become one with the garden is to feel the beating heart of the earth. You are no longer the lonely ape, no longer the great exception to nature as a human being; you are nature's partner and humble supplicant, just like any other creature. Garden for a while, and you develop nearly as intimate an understanding of the passing of the seasons as that of the wild birds overhead. You not only observe the annual cycle of death and renewal, you participate in it—and possibly even take a lesson for your own life from it regarding the limited duration of even the most wintery moods. You cannot help but feel a sense of belonging that the religious, I suppose, find in church.

But it's not just a happy relationship with the birds, bees, and soil microbes that arises out of the vegetable garden—there's the possibility of a happy relationship with human beings, too. Will Rogers once said, "I never met a man I didn't like." I'm not as kindly as Will Rogers, but I can definitely say this: I've never met a gardener I didn't like.

No matter how different from me they may be, I find that I can always talk to gardeners. Yes, we share an interest, but the sense of community among gardeners runs deeper than the common topic of conversation and transcends vastly different ways of living. The respect for nature and the confidence that comes from shaping a piece of earth make gardeners at bottom alike. And even the most worldly gardeners recognize a sense of the miraculous in each other.

So gardening has given me a community of friends across the country, as the Internet turns many people who really care about gardening into a small, gossipy village. It's given me a community at home, too, as Martha and I exchange all-important information about what variety tastes best, and another mom and I stumble through the creation of a school garden to thrill a bunch of 7- and 8-year-olds.

Gardens create ties that bind, which is why a new breed of young community activist is using gardens to reshape cities and towns across the country. Ashley Atkinson of Detroit's Garden Resources Program Collaborative, who has networked and inspired almost a thousand gardeners in her troubled city, told me, "I used to have the foolish idea that urban gardening was all about the food. Now, I think that food is only a small part of it. Gardening here is about beautification, community building, friendship."

In Detroit, where the worst of America's social and economic problems have been playing out for the last 50 years at least—so much so that a good percentage of the city's housing stock has been burned to the ground or abandoned and bulldozed—gardening is a way of reclaiming this vacant land and wringing some meaning out of devastation. It is allowing a grassroots renaissance led by people who have very little money and power, but love to spare for their hometown.

But you don't have to visit Detroit, at the very far end of the American experience, to understand that gardening changes everything. Gardening everywhere is about taking charge, and turning hopelessness and powerlessness into joy. Could there possibly be a more perfect physical expression for the transformation of apathy into creativity than a patch of unused lawn that one day is made into a vegetable garden?

And in a world where so much is beyond the control of any one of us—as much as I'd like to, I cannot personally rid us of the internal combustion engine and replace it with something less noisy or dirty or less likely to turn a beautiful landscape into a field of asphalt—there is a lot of pleasure to be had in reshaping the little piece of earth that is under our control. Thanks to my garden, I can take a small stand against everything I find witless, lazy, and ugly in our civilization and propose my own more lively alternative.

Finally, my vegetable garden makes me happy because it is beautiful, and it says that life is beautiful. There are few things lovelier than a vegetable garden at dusk, and few things more satisfying than going out in the evening to pick the food you've grown before dinner with family and friends. To share the fruits of your labor is to give your love to the people you care most about.

It doesn't matter how much ease or convenience or microwaveability you offer me. I wouldn't trade that experience for anything in the world.

ACKNOWLEDGMENTS

Thanks, Mom, for teaching me that fresh food and good food are one and the same.

Thanks also to the first friends I made in Washington County for showing me what a civilized life really is, especially Bob Nunnelly and Gerald Coble, and Pat Towers and the late Bob Towers—but also Martha Culliton and Erich Kranz, Peg Winship and Doug Reed, Janet and George Scurria, Connie Kheel, Annie and Dave Townsend, Tim Smith, and Nancy and David Higby.

Thanks to David D'Alessandro, Steve Burgay, and Becky Collet for making the perennial writer's problem—how to earn a living—such a source of enlightenment and laughs over the years.

Thanks to my partners at *Garden Rant*—Elizabeth Licata, Amy Stewart, and Susan Harris—for making up the smartest possible kitchen cabinet. Thanks to Lisa Kogan for excellent advice and constant comedy. Thanks to Jeff Gillman, the rare scientist who can really write, for his thoughtful review of the book.

Thanks to my agent Michelle Tessler for being such an absolute pro. Thanks to Gena Smith and Colin Dickerman at Rodale for sharpening up my book and giving me the chance to say what I think.

Thanks most of all to Jeff for his adventuresome palate, intolerance of whining, and calm conviction that his wife is capable of doing anything she sets her mind to.

SUGGESTED READING

Boorstin, Daniel J. *The Americans: The Democratic Experience.* New York: Random House, 1973.

Chalker-Scott, Linda. *The Informed Gardener.* Seattle: University of Washington Press, 2008.

——. *The Informed Gardener Blooms Again.* Seattle: University of Washington Press, 2010.

Csikszentmihalyi, Mihaly. *Flow: The Psychology of Optimal Experience.* New York: Harper Perennial Modern Classics, 2008.

Damrosch, Barbara. *The Garden Primer.* New York: Workman, 2008.

Forty, Adrian. *Objects of Desire: Design and Society Since 1750.* New York: Thames & Hudson, 1992.

Fukuoka, Masanobu. *The One-Straw Revolution: An Introduction to Natural Farming.* New York: New York Review Books, 2009.

Gillman, Jeff. *The Truth about Organic Gardening: Benefits, Drawbacks, and the Bottom Line.* Portland, OR: Timber Press, 2008.

——. *The Truth about Garden Remedies: What Works, What Doesn't, and Why.* Portland, OR: Timber Press, 2008.

Hoy, Suellen. *Chasing Dirt: The American Pursuit of Cleanliness.* New York: Oxford University Press, 1995.

Jackson, Kenneth T. *Crabgrass Frontier: The Suburbanization of the United States.* New York: Oxford University Press, 1985.

Kunstler, James Howard. *The Long Emergency: Surviving the Converging Catastrophes of the Twenty-First Century.* New York: Atlantic Monthly Press, 2005.

Levenstein, Harvey A. *Paradox of Plenty: A Social History of Eating in Modern America.* Berkeley and Los Angeles: University of California Press, 2003.

Mann, Charles C. "Our Good Earth." *National Geographic* (September 2008), 80–107.

McGee, Harold. *On Food and Cooking: The Science and Lore of the Kitchen.* New York: Scribner, 2004.

Mumford, Lewis. *The City in History: Its Origins, Its Transformations, and Its Prospects.* New York: Harcourt Brace Jovanovich, 1961.

Nardi, James B. *Life in the Soil: A Guide for Naturalists and Gardeners.* Chicago: University of Chicago Press, 2007.

Perényi, Eleanor. *Green Thoughts: A Writer in the Garden.* New York: Modern Library, 2002.

Pollan, Michael. *The Omnivore's Dilemma: A Natural History of Four Meals.* New York: Penguin Press, 2006.

Roberts, Paul. *The End of Food.* New York: Houghton Mifflin, 2008.

Sachs, Jessica Snyder. *Good Germs, Bad Germs: Health and Survival in a Bacterial World.* New York: Hill and Wang, 2007.

Schneider, Elizabeth. *Vegetables from Amaranth to Zucchini: The Essential Reference.* New York: William Morrow, 2001.

Seymour, John. *The Self-Sufficient Life and How to Live It.* New York: DK Publishing, 2004.

Shepherd, Gordon M. "Smell images and the flavour system in the human brain." *Nature* 444(7117):316–21.

Stamets, Paul. *Mycelium Running: How Mushrooms Can Help Save the World.* Berkeley, CA: Ten Speed Press, 2005.

Stewart, Amy. *The Earth Moved: On the Remarkable Achievements of Earthworms.* Chapel Hill, NC: Algonquin Books, 2004.

Wolfe, David W. *Tales from the Underground: A Natural History of Subterranean Life.* Cambridge, MA: Perseus, 2001.

INDEX

A

Alexander, William, 27–28
Andrews, Asenath, 145–47
Animal life
  pests, control of, 31–33, 41
  pleasure of contact with, xi–xii
  waste and remains, health
    concerns, 96–97
Anticipation, beauty of in garden, 121
Arugula, 51, 57–58
Asparagus, 51, 142

B

Bacteria in soil, 70–71, 95–98, 100,
  101, 190–91
Beans, 58–59, 62–63, 126, 128–129
Beginning a garden, 29–39. *See also*
  Success, rules for
  author's reasons for, ix–xii
  design principles for aesthetics,
    122–31
  expectations, moderation of, 174–75
  experience, value of, 18
  fencing, 33–34
  grass/sod removal, 35, 36–37
  land requirements, 29–30
  paths and beds, establishment of,
    37–38
  raised-frame gardens, 38–39
  seeds, choosing, 56–57
  size of garden, 30–31, 33–34

  soil enrichment, 35–36
  as voyage of self-discovery, 17
Blight, crop rotation and, 159
Bone density, gardening and, 77–79
Borlaug, Norman, father of Green
  Revolution, 182–83
Brussels sprouts, 61–62
Burpee, W. Atlee, garden seed com-
  pany, 23, 26, 53

C

Catherine Ferguson Academy garden,
  145–47
Childhood memories of gardens,
  114–15
Children
  controlling diet of, 134, 141–42
  obesity in, 140–41
  personal garden section for, 132–33,
    147
Children, benefits of gardening for
  awareness of food quality, 136–40
  improved diet, 133–35, 141–42
  increased contact with nature,
    142–44
  increase in dietary range, 135–36
  Lake Avenue Elementary School
    Garden Club, 133, 148–49,
    161
  moral education, 144
  scientific knowledge, 144–45
Civil War, disease prevention in, 87–89